Christianity in the Arab World

El Hassan bin Talal
Crown Prince of Jordan

With a Preface by
His Royal Highness the Prince of Wales

SCM PRESS LTD

0 334 02729 2

First published 1998 by
SCM Press Ltd
9–17 St Albans Place London N1 0NX

Typeset by Regent Typesetting, London

Printed in Great Britain by
Biddles Ltd, Guildford and King's Lynn

Contents

Foreword by His Royal Highness
The Prince of Wales

Jordan has long been conspicuous as a land of tolerance and peaceful coexistence between people of different faiths. These habits constitute a tradition which has the support of its people quite as much as its Royal Family. Jordan remains a place where ordinary Christians and Muslims have the easy familiarity with, and respect for, each other's beliefs and festivals – *eids* – which once were commonplace throughout the Middle East, and are now sadly so eroded by political and religious strife, and social dislocation.

Of all Jordan's people, nobody has been more steadfast in his support for this priceless tradition than her Crown Prince, Hassan bin Talal. This book is both the latest evidence of this and a particularly important staging post in a long and sometimes, I am sure, exhausting campaign; to promote the understanding without which lasting tolerance cannot be maintained.

The Christian Arab, properly integrated into both wider Middle Eastern society and the Christian world, should be one of the great guarantors of lasting mutual comprehension and trust between two great religions – and more broadly between Islam and the West, as I have sometimes put it. Sadly, neither side seems often to realize that he exists, and when remembered he is increasingly abused, by fundamentalist Christians from abroad as well as fundamentalist Muslims at home.

The Crown Prince writes that 'Muslim Arabs need to know more about the Christians who have historically lived in their midst', and his book was originally intended for that audience. Writing in England, it is equally clear to me that Western Christians need to know more about those of their co-religionists who have lived in that part of the world where Christianity began *since* it began. How many of us realize, for example, that the people of the small town of Ma'adaba in Jordan are the direct descendants of some of the earliest Christians – with a continuous tradition of worship much longer than our own?

It is for this reason that I so welcome the appearance of this book in a British edition. It can do something to relieve our ignorance too. Speaking in Oxford in 1993, I suggested that the degree of misunderstanding between the Islamic and Western worlds remained dangerously high. I tried to draw attention to our debt to Islamic learning; the particular qualities of the Islamic world view; and some of our more glaring misconceptions about Islamic law and practices. I wanted to begin to lessen that misunderstanding.

The overwhelmingly positive response I received showed that the message was timely, and struck a chord. The Crown Prince's account of Christianity in the Arab world is a further and much weightier contribution to the vital task of building understanding, and a work of scholarship which I cannot hope to emulate. I salute him for it, and commend it to the widest possible readership: there can be few subjects which more urgently deserve our attention.

HRH The Prince of Wales

Introduction to the British Edition

First published in English and Arabic by the Royal Institute for Inter-Faith Studies in Amman, Jordan, this book represents a Muslim Arab leader's appreciation of the Christian Arabs. It was originally written to brief Muslim and other Middle Eastern readers of English and Arabic on the nature of Christianity and Christian religious institutions, with particular emphasis on the historical development of the Eastern Christian tradition in the Muslim Arab milieu, and the standing of Christians in Arab society today. The book, however, came to be in much wider demand because of the paucity of easily accessible information on the subjects that it treats. Hence the interest repeatedly expressed to have the book brought out in British and other international editions.

To Muslims having the best interests of Islam in mind, the Christians of the Muslim world – who are essentially the Christian Arabs – are especially important. In mediaeval times, they provided Islam with its principal means of access to the Greek and Hellenistic heritage, and also enriched Arab and Muslim civilization by original contributions in a wide variety of fields. During the long period of Muslim and Arab decline, they helped preserve the Arab heritage from extinction; and during the nineteenth century and the early twentieth, they played the pioneer role in smoothing the Arab transition from traditional to modern ways, and subsequently became the leading indigenous interpreters of Arabism and Islam to the external world. For all their contributions, past and present, the Christian Arabs are richly deserving of the sort of Muslim Arab tribute that this book represents.

The Arab Christian tradition, however, is also deserving of historical understanding and appreciation independently of its importance to Muslims or to Islam. The local roots of this tradition go back to Christianity's earliest days, antedating Islam in the area by more than six centuries. Those were the centuries that witnessed the development of Christian theology, the growth of the universal Christian church and the division of this church into different communions – among them those that survive in the Arab lands to the present day.

It is the author's firm belief that Muslim Arabs need to know more about the Christians who have historically lived in their midst, and the different traditions these Christians represent, the better to understand the rich heritage they hold with them in common. Just as important, to his mind, is the need for Arab and other Muslims to know more about Christianity in general, in a world where people of different faiths can no longer afford to ignore one another. In this respect, however, what applies to the Muslims equally applies to the Christians.

If Muslims need to gain a better knowledge and appreciation of Christianity, and more particularly of the traditions of the Christians living in their midst, so Christians in Europe and the Western world need to gain a better knowledge and appreciation of Islam, and of the culture of the Muslims now living along them, with its rich and many-sided heritage.

The present book, as already indicated, is essentially a Muslim Arab tribute to the Christian Arabs, perhaps long overdue. What still remains overdue, however, is a Christian European tribute to Islam done in the same positive spirit. It is by such exchanges of tribute, supplementing the ongoing Christian–Muslim dialogue, that the cause of interfaith and intercultural understanding in the world can best be promoted and served.

Acknowledgments

The research for this book was done with the diligent assistance of the staff of the Royal Institute for Inter-Faith Studies in Amman. I am particularly indebted to Kamal Salibi, the Director of the Institute, for his help and advice. Special thanks are also due to Gina Anderson, who checked the final draft, and to Randa Salti, Khairi Janbek and Ala'a Resheq, who saw the book through the press and prepared its index.

All Biblical quotations in this book are taken from the *Good News Bible: The Bible in Today's English Version,* translated from the original languages and published by the United Bible Societies.

I

What is Christianity?

The Christian religion maintains that Jesus of Nazareth, conceived of the Holy Spirit, born of the Virgin Mary (between 7 BC and AD 7), dying on the cross in Jerusalem (AD 29 or 30) for the salvation of humanity, rising from the grave on the third day, ascending to heaven, and promising to remain with the world until the end of time (Matthew 28.20), manifests the complete revelation of God to mankind.

This belief is the essence of what Christians call the 'gospel' (Greek *euangelion),* meaning the 'good news', the term being also used in a more concrete sense to denote the accounts of the earthly career and teachings of Jesus written by (or attributed to) the 'apostles' Matthew, Mark, Luke and John (from the Greek *apostolos,* 'one who is sent out' to deliver a message). Those are the four 'canonical' or accepted Gospels, as distinct from a number of 'apocryphal' ones whose authority is rejected.

Christian doctrine, however, does not derive from these four Gospels alone, but also from other accepted apostolic writings, all of them, like the Gospels, originally written in *koine,* the amalgam of Greek dialects which was the *lingua franca* of the Roman world. Those comprise an account of the preaching missions of the disciples of Jesus, written by the author of the Gospel of Luke and called Acts of the Apostles; a selection of twenty-one 'epistles', or letters, addressed by various apostles (thirteen of them by Paul) to their followers, and elaborating the basis of Christian belief and practice; also, a record of apocalyptic visions attributed to the apostle John, and entitled Revelation. The oldest of these Christian scriptures appear to be the epistles of Paul, who died in Rome (probably executed) in c. AD 67, towards the end of the reign of the Roman emperor Nero. The canonical Gospels, written between c. AD 70 and c. AD 100, were apparently composed largely under the influence of Paul's teaching, whose precepts they reflect to varying degrees.

The selection of the scriptures of the Christian canon, and the development of the doctrines that were to gain wider acceptance as Christian 'orthodoxy' (Greek *ortho-doxia*, meaning 'right opinion'), was the work of the church fathers: religious leaders and teachers, revered for their spiritual eminence and personal sanctity, who elaborated the tenets of the Christian faith between the first and eighth centuries AD. The writings of these church fathers form the corpus of what is called patristic literature.

Formally, however, the definition of Christian ortho-doxy, as accepted by the Roman state starting from the reign of Constantine the Great, was undertaken by a succession of seven 'ecumenical' councils of the Christian church (from the Greek *oikoumenikos*, meaning 'belonging to the whole inhabited world'). These were: 1. the first council of Nicaea (325); 2. the first council of Constantinople (381); 3. the council of Ephesus (431); 4. the council of Chalcedon (451); 5. the second council of Constantinople (553); 6. the third council of Constantinople (680); 7. the second council of Nicaea (787).

On the authority of its scriptures, Christianity accepts Jesus as the true Messiah of Israel: the 'Christ' (Greek *Christos,* translating the Hebrew *mashiyah,* meaning the 'anointed' of God) who came to the world to redeem not only his own people, but also all humanity (Isaiah 60.3), in fulfilment of biblical prophecy. Christians further regard the historical, human person of Jesus as the Son of God, sharing the divinity and eternity of God the Father. On the authority of the Gospel of John (1.1–18), he is perceived as the eternal Word (Greek *Logos)* of God become 'flesh' (i.e. a human being) and living as a man, full of grace and truth, and making visible to the world the glory he received as the Father's only Son.

On this basis, and also on the authority of the Gospel of Matthew (28.19) and Paul's Second Epistle to the Corinthians (13.13), God, in Christianity, is perceived as an indivisible 'Holy Trinity' in which three divine components (Greek *hypostasis,* meaning 'substance, nature, essence') stand united: the 'Father', who is God in transcendence; the 'Son', who is God as the Christ; and the 'Holy Spirit', which is God as the divine agency in the universe, which spoke historically through the prophets of Israel, manifests itself perpetually in the fellowship of saints, and constitutes the everlasting bond between the divine and the human in the world. The orthodox definition of the Holy Trinity was authoritatively established in 325 by the council of Nicaea, and forms part of the 'Nicene Creed', the original version of which was refined in 381 by the first council of Constantinople.

Christianity, like Judaism, considers the thirty-nine books of the canonical Hebrew Bible to be the revealed and immutable word of God. (This Hebrew Bible is composed of the Pentateuch or 'five books' of the *Torah,* meaning 'instruction', which embody the Law of Moses, called in Greek the *Nomos;* the twenty-one books of the *Nabhi'im,* or 'prophets'; and thirteen other books called the *Kethubhirn,* or sacred 'writings', among them the devotional book of Psalms.) While the Jews, however, accept the contents of the Hebrew Bible as a set of life rules, to be interpreted in the light of oral traditions and teachings (an 'oral' *Torah)* which, starting from the second century AD, went into the formation of their *Talmud* (Late Hebrew *talmudh,* meaning 'teaching') and *Midrash* (Hebrew *midhrash,* meaning scriptural 'explanation'), Christians interpret this same Hebrew canon in the light of their own scriptures as being basically prophecy relating to the coming of Jesus as the Christ.

In these Christian scriptures, the Hebrew canon is depicted as representing an 'old testament', or 'old covenant' (Greek *palaia diatheke,* II Corinthians 3.14), as distinct from the 'new testament', or 'new covenant' *(kaine diatheke,* Matthew 26.28; Mark 14.24; Luke 2.20; I Corinthians 11.25; II Corinthians 3.6) which supersedes it without putting its validity as divine revelation into question. It might be noted here that the term Judaism (Greek *Ioudaismos),* to denote the Jewish religion as distinct from the Christian, first appears in the writings of Paul (Galatians 1.13). As for the term 'Christianity' (Greek *Christianismos),* to denote the Christian religion as distinct from the Jewish, it first appears in the writings of Ignatius, bishop of Antioch (died c. 110), who was one of the

Apostolic Fathers (the early church fathers who were the immediate successors of the apostles).

With respect to the Christian use of the terms 'old testament' and 'new testament', some explanation is necessary at this point. In ordinary parlance, the Old Testament, to Christians, is the Hebrew Bible which they share with the Jews, while the New Testament is the common name for the Greek scriptures of the Christian canon. In Christian doctrine, however, the term 'old testament' refers, more specifically, to the original 'covenant', or agreement, first concluded between God (called *Yahweh*, or 'Jehovah', and referred to as 'the Lord') and his 'chosen people' in the days of Abraham, then renewed in the days of Moses, to become a pact defining the relations between God and the people of Israel, in accordance with the Ten Commandments revealed to Moses on Mount Sinai (Exodus 5.1–22), these commandments forming the basis of the *Nomos,* or divine Law. The special 'sign' of this 'old testament' was the circumcision of all male Israelites on the eighth day after birth (Genesis 17.9–14), to distinguish them physically from the 'Gentiles' (Hebrew *goyim,* meaning other 'nations'). The term 'new testament', on the other hand, as it features in the Gospels and the epistles of Paul, describes what Christians regard as the new covenant between God and the whole of humanity, which replaced the original covenant between God and Israel. This new covenant was concluded not through prophetic agency, but by the actual coming of the only Son of God to the world as the Christ Jesus (or Jesus Christ), to die on the cross, and by his death redeem not only the people of Israel, but all mankind by an act of divine 'grace' (Greek *charis):* a free favour or gift which becomes operative through confessed faith. Christianity teaches that with the advent of this 'new testament', the application of the Law *(Nomos)* of the 'old testament' ceased to be binding. This teaching, from which derives the basic distinction between Christianity and Judaism, was first developed in the writings of Paul, being summed up in full clarity in his epistle to the Galatians (3.23–25):

> Before the time for faith came, the Law kept us all locked up as prisoners until this coming faith should be revealed . . . the Law was in charge of us until Christ came, in order that we might then be put right with God through faith. Now that the time for faith is here, the Law is no longer in charge of us.

The 'new testament' of Christianity is considered to have been sealed by the blood that flowed from the body of the Christ Jesus as he was nailed on the cross; and its sign was not to be physical circumcision, but the symbolic circumcision of the 'heart', which was 'the work of God's Spirit, not of the written Law' (Paul's epistle to the Romans, 2.28–29).

Unlike the other apostles, who had been personal disciples of Jesus, Paul had probably never known Jesus in life, and was actually an ardent Jewish persecutor of the original followers of Jesus by his own confession (Galatians 1.13–14). The special 'gospel' he began to preach in about AD 40, which transformed Christianity from a narrow Israelite cult into a religion of universal dimensions, was not the 'gospel' preached by the other apostles, but one which Paul received in person by a special 'revelation' (Galatians 1.12), which he describes as follows (II Corinthians 12. 1b–4):

I will now talk about visions and revelations given me by the Lord. I know a certain Christian man who fourteen years ago was snatched up to the highest heaven (I do not know whether this actually happened or whether he had a vision – only God knows). I repeat, I know that this man was snatched to Paradise (again, I do not know whether this actually happened or whether it was a vision – only God knows), and there he heard things which cannot be put into words, things that human lips may not speak.

It was in accordance with his special revelation that Paul set out to articulate the concept of Jesus as the eternal Christ, the Son of God and redeemer of all mankind, before whom Israelites and Gentiles were equal candidates for divine redemption, or salvation, on the basis of faith, and faith alone ('For it is by our faith that we are put right with God; it is by our confession that we are saved', Romans 10.10). But the preaching of Paul was resisted by the apostles who had been disciples of Jesus, and whose concept of the Christhood of Jesus differed radically from his, being closer to the Jewish concept of the Messiah.

In the Hebrew Bible, the term *mashiyah* was first used to describe the kings of Israel (Saul, then David and his descendants), whose kingship over all Israel, then over Judah, was formally consecrated by having their heads anointed with oil, as a sign of divine grace. Later, as the Davidic monarchy became more given to worldly compromise, and more so, after the kingdom of Judah was destroyed (c. 586 BC) and its people carried away to captivity in Babylonia, a succession of Israelite prophets announced the coming of a divinely ordained *mashiyah*: a prince of the line of David, who would redeem the people of Israel from their plight and restore the divine order to the world. And in some of these Messianic prophecies, there was some subtle insinuation that this same Israelite *mashiyah* would also be the redeemer of willing Gentiles. (Isaiah 60.3, for example, speaking of the glory to be achieved by Jerusalem with the advent of the Messiah, remarks that 'Nations will be drawn to your light, and kings to the dawning of your day.')

When Jesus, whose descent from David in the male line was traced through his father Joseph, the husband of Mary (Matthew 1.1–16; Luke 3.23–31), began to preach the coming of the 'kingdom of God' in Palestine, he was accepted by his followers as a *mashiyah* in this Old Testament sense: a rightful claimant to the kingship of Israel, and a potential redeemer of its people, and of others who may be willing to join ranks with them and become Israelites by accepting circumcision. (The original followers of Jesus do not appear to have made an issue of his virgin birth, the scriptural authority for which rests exclusively on Matthew 1.18–25 and Luke 2.1–7.) After the death of Jesus on the cross, his Israelite or 'Hebrew' followers, called the 'Nazarenes', organized themselves in Jerusalem as a special sect (Greek *hodos,* or 'way'), first under his brother James *(Ya'qob bar Yoseph,* or 'Jacob son of Joseph'), then under other members of his family, all of them accepted as descendants of David in the male line, suspected by the Romans of having royal pretensions, and subjected to occasional persecution for this reason (Eusebius, *The Ecclesiastical History,* 3, 19, 20). Church historians refer to James and his successors as the 'bishops of the Circumcision' (Eusebius 4, 5), not only because they were themselves circumcised Israelites, but also because the sect or 'church' they headed regarded itself as being essentially an Israelite communion, priding itself on its strictness in following the Law of Moses, and making circumcision mandatory on all Gentile converts to its 'way'. The Jews considered the Nazarenes as an aberrant Jewish sect, classifying them as *minim,* meaning 'schismatics, heretics'. Apart from recognizing Jesus as the Messiah of biblical promise, which the Jews did not, these Nazarenes differed little from the Jews, being as strict as the strictest among them in adhering to every detail of the Mosaic *Nomos.* Though organized as a special sect or 'church' (Greek *ekklesia,* meaning 'assembly'), they continued to worship in Jewish synagogues until about AD 80, when the Jewish authorities forbad the *minim* the use of their synagogues. In AD 135, when the Roman emperor Hadrian banished all Jews from Jerusalem, the Nazarenes of the city were banished along with them, apparently on the basis that they were no more than a Jewish sect. And it was with their banishment from Jerusalem, in that year, that the line of the 'bishops of the Circumcision' came to an end. In the words of J. Spencer Trimingham, theirs was a 'pathetic Jerusalemite messianic sect',[1] and its passing enhanced rather than hindered the chances for Christianity to spread.

The tenets of the sect, however, survived for some centuries among Christian sectarians, some retaining the name of 'Nazarenes' and denying the virgin birth of Jesus; others called the 'Ebionites' (Hebrew *ebyonim,* meaning 'poor men', apparently because they set high value on

1. J. Spencer Trimingham, *Christianity among the Arabs in Pre-Islamic Times,* London 1979, 48.

asceticism). Apart from their practice of the initiation rite of baptism (from the Greek *baptizein,* to 'immerse' in water), not much is known about the beliefs and religious discipline of these 'Jewish Christians', as they are commonly called. The Carthaginian theologian Tertullian (c. 160 – c. 230), speaking of the Ebionites, reports that they 'make of [Christ] a mere man, although more glorious than the prophets, in that they say that an angel was in him' *(De Carne Christi,* 14, 5). The church historian Eusebius of Caesarea (c. AD 260 – c. 340) describes them as 'holding that they must observe every detail of the Law', rather than seek salvation for themselves 'by faith in Christ alone' (3, 27). St Jerome (c. 340–420), who lived much of his life in Palestine, became acquainted with a community of Ebionites inhabiting Peraea (Transjordan), and could not decide whether they were to be classed as Christians or as Jews (Epistle 112 *ad Augustus,* ch.13). Their special scriptures, which are believed to have been written in Aramaic, have not been discovered as yet, and may have been irretrievably lost.

Such Jewish Christians, possibly of the Ebionite persuasion, still existed in Arabia (as perhaps in other marginal parts of the Christian world) in the days of the Prophet Muhammad. In Arabic, they were called *Nasara,* which was also the Arabic appellation for the Christians in general. From the Qur'an, one learns that the true *Nasara* recognized Jesus as a Messiah (Arabic *masih),* the son of the Virgin Mary by the Holy Spirit (a doctrine which the Qur'an fully endorses), and a prophet to Israel, without attributing divinity to his person, as other *Nasara* did, or conceiving of the One God as a Trinity; also, that the scriptures of these true *Nasara* were a 'gospel' (Arabic *injil,* in the singular). From Muslim tradition, one learns that this *injil* of the *Nasara* was not written in Greek, but in *al-'Ibraniyya*: in the Arabic usage of the period, a term denoting Hebrew as well as Aramaic, which were commonly written in the same script. The Qu'ran commends the sincerity and modesty of the true *Nasara,* and the affection they demonstrated towards the nascent Muslim community, whose concept of Jesus as a human Christ endowed with the Holy Spirit did not differ much from theirs. Muslim tradition depicts the priests and the pious among the *Nasara* as wearing white, apparently as a sign of purity.

The Christianity that survived to become a world religion, however, was not that of the Nazarene *hodos* and its subsequent proliferations, but that of Paul. From the very start of his apostolic career, Paul had clashed with the Nazarene apostles in Jerusalem over the question as to whether or not the advent of Jesus as the universal Christ of all time had superseded the *Nomos,* or Mosaic Law, so that Gentiles could accept the 'gospel' and become Christian without being required to undergo circumcision. And as no agreement could be reached on this matter, the two sides finally reached a parting of ways. Paul and his companions were left to preach their special interpretation of Christianity to the Gentiles throughout the Roman world and its peripheries, while the Jerusalem apostles (James, Peter, John and their companions) continued to restrict their work to Jewish circles (Galatians 2.6–10). (Of the Jerusalem apostles, Peter, it appears, was the one best disposed toward Paul's teaching and prepared to co-operate with him.) Enjoying the privilege of Roman citizenship (Acts 22.25–29; 23.27), Paul could move freely around the Roman world by land and sea, under the protection of Roman law. And unlike the Jerusalem apostles, who were simple folk, Paul was a highly cultivated man, well versed in the Hebrew scriptures, and commanding a knowledge of many languages. From his first preaching base in Damascus, a succession of travels took him first to Arabia, then to different parts of Syria, Anatolia and Greece, and finally to Rome. And wherever he visited, he founded churches which he continued to instruct and advise by written correspondence until the end of his life. His last letters were written from prison in Rome, as he awaited execution. The success of Paul's mission was largely due to the fact that his interpretation of Christianity was a highly intelligent one, having more universal appeal and spiritual substance to offer than the narrow Israelite messianism of the Jerusalem apostles. Other contributing factors were his sincerity, unlimited patience and tireless energy; also, his worldly wisdom, which made him try his best to make the Christianity he preached compatible with Roman state authority. In one passage of his epistle to the Romans (13.1–6), he writes:

> Everyone must obey state authorities, because no authority exists without God's permission, and the existing authorities have been put there by God. Whoever opposes the existing authority opposes what God has ordered; and anyone who does so will bring judgment on himself. For rulers are not to be feared by those who do good, but by those who do evil. Would you like to be unafraid of the man in authority? Then do what is good, and he will praise you because he is God's servant working for your own good. But if you do evil,

you will be afraid of him, because his power to punish is real. He is God's servant and carries out God's punishment on those who do evil. For this reason you must obey the authorities – not because of God's punishment, but also as a matter of conscience. That is why you pay taxes, because the authorities are working for God when they fulfil their duties. Pay, then, what you owe them; pay them your personal and property taxes, and show respect and honour for them all.

It was apparently Paul who instituted the Eucharist (Greek *eucharistia*, 'gratitude'), or Lord's Supper (also called Communion), as the principal Christian rite (I Corinthians 11.23–26; cf. Matthew 26.26–29; Mark 14.22–25; Luke 22.14–20):

For I received from the Lord the teaching that I passed on to you: that the Lord Jesus, on the night he was betrayed, took a piece of bread, gave thanks to God, broke it, and said, 'This is my body, which is for you. Do this in memory of me.' In the same way, after the supper he took the cup and said, 'This cup is God's new covenant, sealed with my blood. Whenever you drink it, do so in memory of me.' This means that every time you eat this bread and drink from this cup, you proclaim the Lord's death until he comes.

Pauline Christianity, however, involved complex theological precepts, not readily understandable, and therefore lending themselves to varied interpretations even in Paul's own time. As Peter put it in his second epistle (II Peter 3.15–16):

> . . . our dear brother Paul wrote to you, using the
> wisdom that God gave him. . . . There are some difficult
> things in his letters which ignorant and unstable people
> explain falsely, as they do with other passages of the
> Scriptures. So they bring on their own destruction.

Hence, from the very beginning, Christianity developed in
a variety of 'heterodoxies' (Greek *heterodoxia,* meaning
'of another opinion'), or 'heresies' (Greek *hairesis,* meaning 'act of choosing'). While some of those heresies (such
as the Nazarene and Ebionite) rejected Paul's authority
altogether, others picked on particular points in Paul's
teachings, to interpret them in gnostic terms (i.e. with a
claim to special esoteric knowledge). By the second
century, for instance, Paul's antinomianism (i.e. his teaching that faith in the 'new testament' liberates the faithful
from the need to observe the Law of the 'old testament')
was being given libertine interpretations by teachers such
as Corinthus, the founder of a gnostic sect which looked
forward to a 'Resurrection of the Kingdom of Christ', to be
followed by a thousand years given up, allegedly, to
'unlimited indulgence in gluttony and lechery at banquets,
drinking-bouts, and wedding-feasts' (Eusebius 3, 28).
Equally licentious, reportedly, was the preaching of a
certain Nicolaus, who maintained that 'the flesh must be
treated with contempt'. It is claimed that his followers, the
Nicolatians, practised 'utter promiscuity', Nicolaus himself offering his wife 'that anyone who wished might have
her' (Eusebius 3, 29).

The same early period witnessed the development of a
range of mystical and ascetical heterodoxies. There were,
for example, the Docetians; among them Monoimus the

Arabian, who advised the search for God within the self. Monoimus reportedly said, 'My God is my mind, my understanding, my soul, my body' (Hippolytus, *The Refutation of All Heresies*).[2] A better known contemporary of Monoimus was Marcion of Pontus (in northern Anatolia), who taught that the God of love of the New Testament could not be identified with the wrathful Creator God of the Old Testament; also, that the Christian gospel was fundamentally incompatible with the Jewish Law. This Marcion broke with the main body of the church, to become the founder of the most successful gnostic sect of that century. Like other gnostics, the Marcionites maintained the dualist distinction between the spirit, representing good, and matter (including the flesh), which they regarded as basically evil. In the ranks of their sect, which appears to have survived in Anatolia, Syria, Arabia and Iraq until the fifth century, the distinction was made between ordinary members, called 'hearers', and an elect group called the 'baptized', or 'initiated', the latter being committed to asceticism and virginity on behalf of the community as a whole. Because they considered humanity basically evil, being matter, the Marcionites denied the essential humanity of Jesus, maintaining that he was a spirit in the form of a man, sent by God to redeem man.

At the opposite extreme were Christian sectarians, such as Beryllus of Bostra, in the Roman province of Arabia, who maintained that Jesus, as the Christ, had 'no divinity of his own, but only the Father's dwelling in him'; also, that he 'did not pre-exist in His own form of being before

---

2. English translation in *The Ante-Nicene Fathers*, Edinburgh, Vol.5, p.122.

He made His home among men' (Eusebius, 6, 33). This view denied the essential divinity of Jesus, as asserted by Paul. (Beryllus was subsequently persuaded to abandon his heterodox teaching and return to orthodoxy.) Meanwhile, during the second and third centuries, there emerged the so-called Monarchian heresies, emphasizing the unity of God at the expense of the doctrine of the Trinity, and explaining that the Father, Son and Holy Spirit were different 'manifestations' or 'aspects' (not essential 'substances') of the one God.

The same centuries that witnessed this proliferation of Judaizing and gnostic Christian sects also witnessed a proliferation of gnostic and other 'apocryphal' Gospels and epistles, supporting one heterodoxy or another (Eusebius 3, 25). But in between the extremes of heterodoxy, the groundwork for a Christian 'orthodoxy' was already being laid by the more sober church fathers. From the very beginning, these fathers saw in excessive theological speculation a threat to the unity of the Christian ranks, and therefore sought to keep such speculation within reasonable bounds.

2

The Origins of the Nicene Creed

The first concern of the church fathers was to determine which of the extant Christian scriptures were to be accepted as the 'canon' (Greek *kanon,* meaning 'measuring rod, rule, criterion') for the orthodox faith. The Gospels of Matthew, Mark, Luke and John seemed to recommend themselves for ready acceptance, along with the available corpus of Pauline epistles and the Acts of the Apostles. The claims to authority of other apostolic writings (notably the epistle to the Hebrews, the three epistles of John, the epistles of James and Jude, and the book of Revelation) were initially doubted, only gaining general acceptance after prolonged hesitation.

The second concern of the church fathers was to establish an acceptable 'creed' (from the Latin *credo,* 'I believe'): a doctrinally correct and complete 'confession' (or declaration) of the Christian faith. The elements for such a creed could indeed be discovered in the Christian scriptures, though nowhere in one passage, with every tenet fully spelt out. For example, and as already observed, the concept of Jesus as the incarnation of the divine Word comes from the introductory chapter of the Gospel of John, while that of his virgin birth rests on the authority of the Gospels of Matthew and Luke. Belief in the resurrection of Christ and his ascension to heaven derives from the authority of the Gospels of Matthew, Mark and Luke, the Acts of the Apostles, and the writings of Paul, the Gospel of John alone not mentioning the ascension. The doctrine of the Holy Trinity, for its part, as already indicated, involves an elaboration of the last words addressed by Jesus to his disciples before his ascension to heaven, as reported in Matthew 28.19 ('Go then, to all the peoples everywhere and make them my disciples: baptize them in the name of the Father, the Son, and the Holy Spirit'); also on the last verse of Paul's second epistle to the Corinthians, 13.13 ('The grace of the Lord Jesus Christ, the love of God, and the fellowship of the Holy Spirit be with you all'). The concepts of the universal or 'catholic' (Greek *katholikos,* meaning 'general') Christian 'church' of the baptism, and of church authority as the agent of divine authority on earth, derives from the words addressed by Jesus to his disiple Peter, as reported in Matthew 16.18–19:

> And so I tell you, Peter: you are a rock, and on this rock foundation I will build my church, and not even death will ever be able to overcome it. I will give you the keys of the Kingdom of heaven; and what you prohibit on earth will be prohibited in heaven, and what you permit on earth will be permitted in heaven.

The closest approximation to a scriptural creed occurs in what appear to be two parts of a hymn quoted by Paul (I Timothy 3.16; II Timothy 2.11–13) to sum up what he considered 'the secret of our religion'. Speaking of the Christ, this hymn says:

He appeared in human form,
was shown to be right by the spirit,
and was seen by the angels.
He was preached among the nations,
was believed in throughout the world,
and was taken up to heaven.
If we have died with him,
we shall also live with him.
If we continue to endure,
we shall also rule with him.
If we deny him,
he also will deny us.
If we are not faithful,
he remains faithful,
because he cannot be false to himself.

Supplementing the theologically pithy content of this hymn is the injunction by Paul to 'confess that Jesus is Lord and believe that God raised him from death' (Romans 10.9). Hence, before being accorded the baptism which admitted them to the ranks of the faithful, candidates for conversion to Christianity came to be asked three questions: 1. Do you believe in God the Father almighty? 2. Do you believe in Jesus Christ his Son, our Lord? 3. Do you believe in the Holy Spirit, in the church, and in the resurrection? Affirmative answers to these questions were taken to amount to an adequate confession of Christian belief, though they did not form a true declaratory creed. But out of the baptismal confession used in Rome in about AD 200, in the form of affirmative answers to set questions, there developed by the fourth century what is known as the Old Roman Creed, of which the so-called 'Apostles' Creed', developed by about AD 500 and still used in Western churches, is a direct descendant. Without going into theological detail, this Roman Creed (of which there were regional variants) affirmed belief in the following:

1. God the Father almighty
    (a) creator of heaven and earth
2. The Lord Christ Jesus His only Son
    (a) born of the Holy Spirit and the Virgin Mary
    (b) crucified under Pontius Pilate[1] and buried
    (c) rose from the dead on the third day
    (d) ascended to heaven
    (e) sits on the right hand of the Father
    (f) thence he shall come to judge the living and the dead
3. The Holy Spirit
4. The Holy Church
5. The remission of sins
6. The resurrection of the flesh

Other creeds elaborated in the meanwhile by different churches, or by particular church fathers, dwelt on finer points of theology, on some of which there was no general agreement. This gave rise to disputes. The most controversial was the creed advanced by the Alexandrian priest Arius (died 336) which, apparently in elaboration of older Monarchian doctrine, described the 'Lord Jesus' as the only 'begotten' Son of the Father, implying a denial of the co-eternity of the Father and the Son in the Holy Trinity. This 'Arian' creed, and the accompanying teaching, gained

---

1. Pontius Pilate was the Roman procurator of Judaea in Palestine c. AD 26–36.

ready acceptance among Christian communities in various parts of the Roman world and its peripheries, resulting in a heresy whose popularity threatened the unity of the Christian church as none before it had done. In the Arian teaching, the Son and (by implication) the Holy Spirit in the Trinity were presented as agents of the Father and created beings, albeit pre-eminent ones. This reduced Christianity, basically, to an evolved form of Jewish monotheism, with the Father as the Creator God who alone was eternal. At the same time, by acknowledging the essential divinity of the Son and the Holy Spirit in the Trinity, Arianism implied a departure from monotheism, effectively recognizing three gods: one primary, and two secondary ones.

The appeal of Arianism rested on its logic: its concept of the 'Father' as being more ancient than the 'Son' of whom he was the progenitor. To the opponents of Arianism, however, Christian belief rested on the premise that the Creator God the Father, the Son as the Father's revelation to mankind, and the Holy Spirit as the divine agency for ever active in the human world, shared the same eternity, as it was in the very nature of God to be Father, Son and Holy Spirit at the same time, a matter that was not subject to ordinary human logic.

It was in the early rage of the Arian controversy that Flavius Valerius Aurelius Constantinus, historically known as Constantine the Great (died 337), was proclaimed Roman emperor in Britain (306), converted to Christianity (312), became sole emperor (324), and moved the Roman capital from the Old Rome, in Italy, to a New Rome on the Bosphorus: the ancient Greek town of Byzantion (in Latin form, Byzantium), which he rebuilt and renamed

Constantinople after his own name (330). Though not the first Roman emperor to be Christian (Philip the Arab, 244–249, had been Christian, although he had observed pagan rites in office), Constantine was the first one to accord Christianity official Roman recognition, thereby initiating the process which resulted in Christianity becoming the established religion of the Roman state under Emperor Theodosius the Great (379–395).

As a Christian, Constantine the Great appears to have been initially of Arian persuasion or sympathy; but no sooner had he become sole emperor than he decided to settle the theological dispute between the Arians and their opponents by summoning a general council of the Christian church to agree on an official definition of Christian orthodoxy. This first ecumenical council was held in the city of Nicaea (today Iznik), in western Anatolia, with the emperor himself participating in the more important sessions. (It was he, reportedly, who suggested the term 'consubstantial', i.e. 'of one substance', to describe the identity in *hypostasis*, or essential nature, between the Father and the Son in the Trinity.) In the deliberations of this First Council (325), the church fathers opposed to Arianism won the day, producing a statement of orthodox Christian belief which was carefully worded under the direction of the emperor, and came to be known as the Nicene Creed. This creed was published in Greek and Latin versions, Latin being the language of the Roman church in the West, while Greek was the language of the churches of the East. At some later time, an expression was introduced into the Latin version – but not the Greek – touching one point of minor significance. Originally, the creed had described the Holy Spirit as proceeding 'from the

Father'. The Latin version subsequently came to describe the same Holy Spirit as proceeding from the Father 'and the Son' (Latin *Filioque*). Initially, little issue was made of this matter.

The publication of the Nicene Creed did not put an end to the Arian controversy, which continued to rage until the end of the century, surviving in some areas for some time thereafter. The persistence of the controversy made it necessary for Theodosius the Great to summon a second ecumenical council at Constantinople in 381 to reassert the principles of Christian orthodoxy. At this Second Council, the text of the original Nicene Creed was subjected to some revision (the same creed was subjected to further elucidation by the Fourth Council held at Chalcedon in 451). Here is the full text of the Nicene Creed in its so-called 'Constantinian' form (i.e, as revised by the Second Council), with the English for the disputed *Filioque* clause in italics:

We believe 1. in one God the Father Almighty, maker of heaven and earth, and of all things visible and invisible. 2. And in one Lord Jesus Christ, the only begotten Son of God, begotten of His Father before all worlds, God of God, Light of Light, very God of very God, begotten, not made, being of one substance with the Father, by whom all things were made; who for us men and for our salvation came down from heaven and was incarnate of the Holy Spirit and the Virgin Mary and was made Man. And was crucified also for us under Pontius Pilate, and suffered and was buried, and He rose again the third day, according to the Scriptures, and ascended into heaven and sits on the right hand of the Father, and

He shall come again to judge the living and the dead, whose kingdom shall have no end. 3. And in the Holy Spirit, the Lord and Giver of Life, who proceeds from the Father *and the Son*, who with the Father and the Son together is worshipped and glorified, who spoke by the Prophets. 4. And in the Catholic and Apostolic Church. 5. We acknowledge one baptism for remission of sins. 6. We look for the resurrection of the dead, 7. and the life of the world to come.

Under the impact of an orthodoxy solidly backed by Roman state authority, the Arian heresy, starting with the reign of Theodosius the Great, began rapidly to lose ground, and ultimately vanished from existence, as did other heresies of the pre-Nicene period. (In Visigothic Spain, Arianism survived until the time of the Arab conquest.) The heterodox Christian teachings on the post-Nicene period were all articulated in Nicene terms, no matter the degree of their departure from orthodoxy.

3

The Organization of the Church

According to the Gospel of John (20.21–22, cf. Matthew 28.16–20, Mark 16.14–18, Luke 24.36–49), Jesus invested his disciples with the Holy Spirit, giving them full authority as his apostles, when he appeared to them in the evening of the day of his resurrection:

> Jesus said to them . . ., 'Peace be with you. As the Father sent me, so I send you.' Then he breathed on them and said, 'Receive the Holy Spirit. If you forgive people's sins, they are forgiven; if you do not forgive them, they are not forgiven.'

Endowed with full spiritual authority by Jesus himself, the apostles passed the Holy Spirit on to their followers by placing their hands on them (Acts 8.17). And it was by such 'laying on of hands' that the apostles' followers, in turn, passed on this same authority to those who succeeded them in the leadership of the 'church'. These were the 'bishops' (Greek *episkopos*, or 'overseer') and 'presbyters' (Greek *presbyteros*, or 'elder'), who were 'ordained' to attend to the churches the apostles had founded, along with 'deacons' (Greek *diakonos*, or 'servant') to assist them in their work. It appears that 'presbyters' or 'elders' were already being appointed by the Nazarene apostles in Jerusalem to assist them in their preaching work before the time of Paul (Acts 11.30). But it was probably Paul who first gave the 'presbytery' the formal organization that made it the forerunner of the Christian priesthood (I Timothy 1.5; 4.14; 5.17; cf. Acts 14.23). It was also Paul, apparently, who first appointed 'bishops' to oversee and direct the work of the 'presbyters' in the churches he founded, and 'deacons' to assist in church service without wielding independent spiritual authority. (The earliest mention of 'bishops' and 'deacons' appears in two of the Pauline epistles: 'bishops' in Philippians 1.1; I Timothy 3.1; II Timothy 1.7 and 'deacons' in Philippians 1.1; I Timothy 3.8–13). Paul, it seems, was not only the originator of the form of Christianity that survived to become a world religion, but also the founder of the 'church' as an organized institution run by a hierarchy of officials to whom apostolic authority was detailed by a formal laying on of hands or 'ordination'. The 'mother church' of Jerusalem, by contrast, was no more than an 'assembly' of the faithful, loosely organized as a *hodos*, or 'way' (i.e. sect), under the leadership of the original apostles, and answering to the dynastic authority of relatives of Jesus whose functions were undefined, and who only later came to be described as 'bishops' by church historians.

The passing of the apostolic age left authority in the different churches in the hands of the bishops who claimed it on the basis that they were the ordained successors of the apostles. These bishops, in their turn, proceeded to ordain Christians of a new generation to church ministry, so that the spiritual authority of the apostles, originally derived

from Jesus himself, was passed on to succeeding generations of church ministers – bishops, presbyters (subsequently called priests) and deacons – in what came to be
regarded as a legitimate 'apostolic succession'. In each
Christian church, ordination to the ranks of the ministry
by the 'laying on of hands' remained the preserve of the
presiding bishop, and was considered a 'sacrament': the
visible sign of an inward grace, distinguishing the 'clergy',
as a class wielding received apostolic authority, from the
common run of the 'laity'. (This distinction between
'clergy' and 'laity', based on the Old Testament distinction
between a special class of 'priests' and 'Levites' [temple
functionaries] and ordinary worshippers, was already
being made in c. AD 95 by Bishop Clement of Rome, one of
the Apostolic Fathers).

Receiving their spiritual authority from the bishops who
ordained them, the priests (but not the deacons), like the
bishops, administered the other church sacraments, of
which the original ones were baptism and the eucharist, or
'Lord's Supper'. By the initiatory sacrament of baptism,
which involved immersion in water, or the application of
water to the body in some manner, followed by an anoint-
ing with 'chrism', or consecrated oil, the baptized were
cleansed of original human sin and so made candidates for
divine grace and salvation through Christ. Originally, as
already observed, converts to Christianity were required to
confess their faith before receiving baptism. But as the
sacrament came to be administered in childhood to
succeding generations of children born to Christian
parents, the rite of 'confirmation' was introduced as a
supplement to baptism, whereby baptized children, as they
approached adolescence, were required to make a public

confession of the faith to which they were born, so as to gain acceptance as members of the church in their own right.

As for the eucharist, or 'Lord's Supper', it was the original sacrament around which church worship revolved. By this sacrament, the presiding priest or bishop offered the body and blood of Christ for the faithful to partake of, in the form of consecrated bread and wine, so they would physically receive grace. The elaborate ritual connected with the administration of the eucharist, differing from one church to another, evolved with time into the form or service called the Mass (Late Latin *missa*, feminine of *missus*, past participle of *mittere*, to send, i.e. the 'sending away' or 'dismissal' at the end of a religious service).

In addition to the three original sacraments of ordination, baptism and the eucharist, others were established in due course. From an early time, the church came to recognize Christian marriage as the sacrament of 'holy matrimony', whereby man and wife became permanently united in one sacred entity. The concept of marriage as a sacrament derives from the authority of Paul (Ephesians 5.31–33):

As the scripture says [Genesis 2.24]: 'For this reason a man will leave his father and mother and unite with his wife, and the two of them will become one.' There is a deep secret truth revealed in this scripture, which I understand as applying to Christ and the church. But it also applies to you: every husband must love his wife as himself, and every wife must respect her husband.

Another sacrament that came to be established with time was penance, consisting of a confession of sin followed by the forgiveness of the sin. This sacrament was based on the authority of the first epistle of John (1 John 1.8–9):

> If we say that we have no sin, we deceive ourselves, and there is no truth in us. But if we confess our sins to God, he will keep his promise and do what is right: he will forgive our sins and purify us from our wrong-doing.

Finally, there was the sacrament of extreme unction, or 'last rites': the prayer and anointment with chrism administered by a priest or bishop to a dying person, or a person in danger of death.

In addition to directing ecclesiastical affairs and ensuring the proper administration of the sacraments (also, correct religious preaching and help to the poor and needy), the bishops in the Christian church were the ultimate repositories of disciplinary power in their respective sees. The threat of 'excommunication', which barred offending individuals or parties from receiving the sacraments, and forbade the faithful to deal with them, normally sufficed to maintain discipline in the ranks of laity and clergy alike. And in cases where the threat did not suffice, excommunication was actually applied, more often than not bringing the recalcitrant to repentance.

The 'Gentile' churches established in the Roman world by Paul and his associates centred upon cities and towns whose names they carried. After the passing of the apostolic age, each of these churches continued under its own bishop. And because urban life was more developed and widespread in the East (peninsular Greece, Asia Minor, Syria and Palestine, Mesopotamia and Egypt) than in the West, the Eastern churches (using Greek) were more numerous than the Western ones (using Latin). Except that the Western church of Rome, being the church of the imperial capital, seems to have enjoyed a certain pre-eminence over the other churches of the empire from the very start. Moreover, while the bishops of the Eastern churches exercised religious authority over areas which were relatively small, those of the West exercised the same authority over larger areas, called 'dioceses' (Latin *diocesis,* from the Greek *dioikesia,* 'housekeeping'), which normally conformed to Roman administrative units. (The Western church borrowed the term 'diocese' from Roman administrative usage, where it denoted an 'administrative division'.) Following the example of the West, the Eastern churches began to apply the term 'diocese' to areas over which bishops wielded religious jurisdiction. In the East as in the West, the diocese consisted of a number of 'parishes' (Latin-Greek *paroicia,* or 'neighbourhood', from the Greek *paroikos,* meaning 'neighbour'): ecclesiastical units, each having its own church and priest, but answering to the same bishop.

The office of a bishop was called a 'see' (Latin *sedes,* or 'seat'), the term being also applied loosely to the diocese under his jurisdiction. By the end of the third century, the 'metropolitan' bishops of Roman provincial capitals began to gain a recognized pre-eminence over the bishops of less important townships of their provinces, from whom they started being distinguished, in the course of the fourth century, by the title of 'archbishop'.

Meanwhile, starting with the third century, the

authority of the bishop of Rome in the West, and the bishops of Alexandria and Antioch in the East, began to gain a recognized acceptance beyond the limits of their original 'sees'. Special respect was also accorded to the bishop of the 'mother church' of Jerusalem, which had been reconstituted as a 'Gentile' communion shortly after the expulsion of the Nazarenes and their 'bishops of the Circumcision' from the city in 135. (According to Eusebius, 5, 12, it was from the time of the siege of the Jews under Hadrian that 'the church there first consisted of Gentiles, who took the place of converts from the Circumcision and were headed by the first Gentile bishop'.) Though founded as late as 330, when Constantine the Great moved the Roman capital to Constantinople, the church of Constantinople, following the Second Council, acquired the standing of an apostolic church equal in pre-eminence to those of Rome, Alexandria and Antioch, on the grounds that Constantine's invaluable service to Christianity had made him the 'equal of the apostles' (Greek *isapostolos*). Thus emerged the concept of the five apostolic sees of the ecumenical Christian church, whose bishops were distinguished by the title of 'patriarch' (Greek *patriarches,* or 'chief father'). (The bishop of Jerusalem was only accorded the rank of patriarch in 451 by the Fourth Council.)

From an early time, bishops who won the hearts of their flock in a special way had been affectionately addressed as *papa*, meaning 'Father'. This appellation, in the West, began to be used by the sixth century to distinguish the patriarch-bishop of Rome from his subordinates, and from the ninth century onwards *papa,* as a title, came to be applied almost exclusively to the patriarch-bishops of

Rome (in English, the 'popes'). (Otherwise, this title only remains in use in Egypt, where it has traditionally been applied to the Coptic patriarchs of Alexandria.)

According to Christian tradition, the church of Rome had been founded jointly by the apostles Peter and Paul, with Peter as its first head, so that the bishops of Rome were his apostolic successors. (Peter was also considered the founder of the church of Antioch, where 'the believers were first called Christians', Acts 11.26; while Mark, a pre-eminent disciple of Paul's and Peter's, was regarded as the apostolic founder of the church of Alexandria.) Conscious of their standing as successors of Peter and Paul, the bishops of Rome considered the guardianship of the apostolic tradition, and the leadership of the ecumenical Christian church, to be their special responsibility. Attempts on their part to intervene in the affairs of other churches date as far back as c. 190, when one Roman bishop threatened to excommunicate an Eastern Christian communion in Anatolia for celebrating Easter on the day of the Jewish Passover, rather than on the Sunday after the full moon that occurs upon or next after the spring equinox (21 March), as was done in Rome. Starting from 256, the Roman bishops began to base their claim to special ecclesiastical authority on the words addressed by Jesus to Peter, describing him as the 'rock foundation' on which the church would be built (Matthew 16.18–19; see above). Between the fourth century and the mid-eleventh, patriarchs of the Eastern churches who remained followers of Christian orthodoxy, as defined by the ecumenical councils, were willing to accord the popes of Rome a special standing as 'first among equals', but no more.

4

The Christological Controversies

By the end of the fourth century, the ecumenical Christian church, with its five apostolic sees, had already taken full form, its creed carefully defined by the First and Second Councils, and backed by Roman imperial authority. In the East, however, theological speculation remained rife in ecclesiastical circles, particularly in the sees of Alexandria and Antioch. Among the theologians of the Alexandrian school, there was a marked tendency to emphasize the divinity of Jesus at the expense of his humanity, while the opposite tendency prevailed in the Antiochene school. The Alexandrian doctrine revolved around the teaching of Apollinaris of Laodicea (active 360–380), who taught that the nature (Greek *physis*) of Christ was essentially divine; i.e. that Christ was God *become* a man, his human nature being no more than a form; accordingly, Christians would be fully justified in conceiving of the Virgin Mary and addressing her in prayer as the *Theotokos,* or 'Mother of God'. This doctrine came to be branded as 'Monophysite' (from the Greek *mone physis,* meaning 'one nature'). The Antiochene doctrine, by contrast, stemming from the teaching of Theodore of Mopsuestia (c. 350–428), emphasized the separateness of the the divine and human natures in Christ, recognizing the humanity of Christ, so to speak, as the receptacle of his divinity. The followers of this school conceived of Christ as God *in* a man, regarding the Virgin Mary as the mother of Christ as a man, and not of Christ as God.

Accordingly, they considered it unacceptable for Mary to be regarded and addressed as the *Theotokos*.

From the point of view of the more cautious of the post-Nicene fathers, both these positions threatened to play havoc with Christian orthodoxy. To concede the claim that Christ was essentially God in human form (which was the Monophysite position) meant accepting that Christ was incapable of true human suffering and death on behalf of mankind, which was the essence of the Christian concept of redemption, as first articulated by Paul. On the other hand, to concede a separateness between the divine and human natures in Christ did not only involve the non-acceptance of Mary as the 'Mother of God'. It also implied that it was only Christ as a man, and not as God, who suffered and died on the cross, which again seriously compromised the concept of redemption.

One theologian of the Antiochene school, Nestorius, went to the extreme of openly denying the 'hypostatic' union between the divine and human 'persons' in Christ. This Nestorius (an Aramaeo-Arab originally from Mesopotamia, then part of the Persian empire) became patriarch of Constantinople in 428, whereupon he tried to establish his doctrine as ecumenical orthodoxy. But he found himself vehemently opposed by the patriarch of Alexandria, Cyril (412–444), who staunchly supported the Monophysite view. To settle the 'Nestorian' controversy, a special ecumenical council (the Third Council, 431) was held at Ephesus in south-western Anatolia; and at this council, Cyril succeeded in getting the Nestorian teaching condemned as a heresy and in having Nestorius himself deposed from his patriarchal see and banished, ultimately to die in exile in the eastern desert of Egypt. Nestorianism, however, survived outside the pale of the Roman Empire, in Mesopotamia and Persia. The Nestorians formally broke off relations with the see of Antloch in 498, whereupon they established themselves as an independent communion under a catholicos (Greek *katholikos*, 'universal, general'), or supreme bishop, residing in Seleucia-Ctesiphon, the capital of the Persian empire on the Tigris river, in what today is Iraq. Between the fifth and seventh or eighth centuries, and possibly until as late as the thirteenth century, Nestorian missionary activity resulted in the sprouting of Nestorian Christian enclaves in inner Asia as far east as China, and also in India and the parts of Africa bordering the Indian Ocean.

Next came the turn of the patriarchs of Alexandria – Cyril and his successor Dioscorus (444–454) – to press their teaching of the 'one nature of the Word incarnate': 'two pharaohs, one succeeding the other'; so it was said of these two powerful and strong-willed Alexandrian patriarchs. The success scored by Cyril at Ephesus had caused considerable alarm in Rome, where the popes began to fear the Alexandrian patriarchs as serious contenders to their own claim to ecclesiastical supremacy over the Christian world. Little wonder, then, that the Roman papacy, under Leo I (Saint Leo, or Leo the Great, 440–461), should have taken the lead in opposing the Monophysite position adopted by the Alexandrian see. A first attempt to settle the resulting controversy by holding another ecumenical council at Ephesus (449) failed.

Arriving at Ephesus with a band of robust monks serving as his bodyguard, Dioscorus easily purged the council of his intimidated opponents, forcing those who remained to adopt a decision in his favour (hence the historical reference to this council as the Robber Synod of Ephesus). Two years later, however, another ecumenical council (the Fourth Council, 451) was convened at Chalcedon (today Kadikoy), on the side of the Bosphorus facing Constantinople. And the outcome of this council, where the papal party enjoyed the support of the emperor Marcian (450–457), was the assertion that Christ had indeed not one, but two natures, each perfect in itself and distinct from the other, yet perfectly united in one person who was God and a man at the same time.

The adoption of this christological formula at Chalcedon amounted to a condemnation of the Monophysite doctrine, although no condemnation was actually expressed in the council decisions. The church fathers meeting at Chalcedon, no less than the Roman (or better, Byzantine) emperor, obviously hoped to avoid an open break with the Alexandrian see, which enjoyed strong popular support not only in Egypt but also in Syria and other parts of the Byzantine empire which were not Greek. It was probably realized already that behind the Egyptian and Syrian persistence in religious dissent lurked ethnic feelings of resentment at the established Greek dominance in the empire.

The Council of Chalceon, however, did result in an immediate break within the church of Alexandria between the 'Copts' or native Egyptians, who stuck to the Monophysite teaching, and the Greek and Hellenized Coptic elements in the country who accepted the Chalcedonian definition of Christian orthodoxy. In Egypt, as in Syria, the latter came to be called the 'Melchites' (probably meaning the partisans of the *malka*, Syriac for 'king', with reference to the Byzantine emperor). Henceforth, two patriarchs were to occupy the Alexandrian see, one Monophysite and Coptic, the other 'Melchite', standing for Chalcedonian orthodoxy. While Byzantine rule over Egypt continued, it was the Melchite patriarchs of the see of Alexandria who actually resided in the city, leaving the Coptic patriarchs to run the affairs of their separate church from one monastery or another in the nearby desert.

In the see of Antioch, as in the see of Alexandria, the conflict between the Chalcedonian and Monophysite parties ultimately led to an ecclesiastical parting of ways. In 512, a Monophysite monk called Severus (died 458) became patriarch of Antioch, only to be overthrown six years later and sent into exile in Constantinople. At Antioch, he was replaced by a representative of the Chalcedonian, Melchite party. The Syrian Monophysites refused to recognize the authority of the new Melchite patriarch, and proceeded to elect a patriarch of their own, Sergius of Tella.

For political reasons, if for no other, the emperors and patriarchs of Constantinople had meanwhile grown convinced of the need to win the Syrian dissenters back to the ecumenical fold. And a serious attempt in that direction was made during the reign of Justinian I (the Great, 527–565), whose wife Theodora was a Monophysite and a friend and protector of Severus. Sensing the relaxed imperial attitude towards them, the Monophysites of Syria seized the opportunity to follow the example of the Copts of Egypt and organize themselves as an independent

'Jacobite' church (543–544). The new communion took its name from the monk Jacob Baradaeus (died 578), one of its early leaders, and a favourite of Theodora's. (Baradaeus was consecrated bishop of Edessa by an exiled Coptic patriarch of Alexandria, after which he proceeded to ordain bishops and priests on his own, thereby laying the foundations for the Jacobite church hierarchy.) Justinian, prompted by his wife Theodora, subsequently summoned the second council of Constantinople (the Fifth Council, 553) to reaffirm the Chalcedonian definition of the Christian faith in principle, while tempering it somewhat in favour of the Monophysites. Thus, the Jacobite church in Syria was allowed to survive, its leaders, like those of the Chalcedonian Melchite communion, continuing to style themselves patriarchs of Antioch, although they did not actually reside in Antioch.

While the Coptic church, in Egypt, replaced Greek with Coptic (a descendant of ancient Egyptian) in their liturgy, the Jacobites replaced Greek with Syriac (the Christian form of ancient Aramaic). Thus, the Coptic communion in Egypt and the Jacobite communion in Syria emphasized their character as ethnic (or what we would today call 'national') churches. But older than both, as a national 'communion' using its own language, was the Armenian church.

Comprising the eastern highlands of Asia Minor, between Roman Anatolia and Persia, Armenia in Roman and Byzantine times was a kingdom whose territory was coveted by powerful imperial neighbours from both sides. The Armenians considered their church an apostolic one, tracing its origins to the preaching of two of the original disciples of Jesus, Thaddaeus and Bartholomew, the first

'Illuminators of Armenia'. But it was only in 301 that Saint Gregory (called the Illuminator) persuaded King Tiridates the Great to establish Christianity as the Armenian state religion (hence the common appellation of the Armenian apostolic church as the 'Gregorian' church). This made the Armenians historically the first Christian nation. Later in the century, as the Roman emperors and the Sassanid kings of Persia agreed to divide the Armenian territory between them, the Armenians were greatly angered by the unconcern of the Roman emperors. who were fellow Christians, for their national independence. Consequently, the Armenian church, which had earlier followed the see of Constantinople, declared its complete break from that see in 365, establishing itself as an independent communion under the see of Echmiadzin (near Yerevan, today the capital of the Armenian Republic). The supreme bishop of the Armenian church remains the Catholicos of Echmiadzin whose cathedral, many times rebuilt, dates from the year 303. From the very beginning, the Armenian church developed a liturgy of its own, using the Armenian language (the Bible was first translated into Armenian in 406.)

The continuing disaffection of the Armenians for Byzantium was no doubt a contributing factor to their subsequent espousal of the Monophysite definition of the Christian faith. At a council held at Dvin in 506, their church rejected the decisions of the council of Chalcedon, and thus became established as a communion openly subscribing to Monophysite teaching.

Of the three Monophysite communions that began to emerge starting from the fifth century, the Jacobites of Syria (who also had a strong presence in Mesopotamia, then part of the Persian empire) were no less active in missionary work than the Nestorians. It was they who brought Christianity in its Monophysite form to different parts of the Indian Ocean basin, such as the Malabar coast of India, and the island of Socotra, off the southern coast of Arabia. (Monophysite Christianity was still established in Socotra when the Portuguese conquered the island in the early sixteenth century; and a self-governing Jacobite communion remains in existence in India to this day.)

Another attempt by the Roman state and church at Constantinople to come to terms with the Monophysites (Copts, Jacobites and Armenians) was made during the reign of the emperor Heraclius (610–641). Shortly after coming to the throne, Heraclius was faced with a Persian invasion and occupation of his Asiatic territories, and also of Egypt. And although the Persians were a non-Christian power aggressing against Christian Roman territory, it became clear to Byzantium that wherever the Persian invaders arrived, they received support (or at least no opposition) from the indigenous Monophysite Christian population. Under the energetic leadership of their emperor, the Byzantines did manage nonetheless to defeat the Persians and fully regain the territories they had earlier lost to them (628). Meanwhile, starting from about 610 and more effectively after 622 (the year marking the start of the Muslim *Hijra* era), the Arabian tribes had come to be united by the Prophet Muhammad (died 632) under the banner of Islam. And the Byzantine forces had hardly begun to re-establish themselves in Syria and Egypt when the Arab forces of Islam, answering to the commands of the Prophet's 'caliphs' (or 'successors') in the Hijazi city of Medina, began rapidly to conquer these two countries.

And once again, to the grave concern of Byzantium, the Monophysites in Syria and Egypt appeared to be actively assisting (certainly, not opposing) a non-Christian conquest of Christian lands.

In the course of his Persian campaigns, Heraclius became keenly aware of the need to appease his Monophysite subjects, and he thought he could easily achieve this by a major doctrinal concession. It appears that shortly before his time, a certain Theodore of Pharan, or Theodore of Arabia (his name is only mentioned in the acts of the Sixth Council of 680) had been preaching the emanation of one 'energy' (Greek *energeia*) and will (Greek *theletis*) from the union of the divine and human natures in Christ. The sources indicate that the followers of this doctrine in Syria were called 'Maronites' after the monastery of Dayr Marun, their religious centre in the valley of the Orontes river, near the town of Hama. (This monastery carried the name of Marun, a Syrian saint active in the late fourth and early fifth centuries.) (According to the tenth-century Arab historian al-Mas'udi, the Maronite church, which came to have its centre in Dayr Marun, was founded during the reign of the Byzantine emperor Maurice, 582–602.) To Heraclius (also to Sergius, the patriarch of Constantinople, and to Honorius, the pope of Rome), this 'Monothelite' (or 'one will') formula, whoever were its original exponents, seemed to offer the ideal grounds for a workable doctrinal compromise between Chalcedonian orthodoxy and Monophysitism. After pressing for its acceptance as orthodox doctrine for some two decades, Heraclius finally issued a decree (the *Ekthesis*, 638) imposing its acceptance by imperial *fiat*.

Rather than solving the problem for the Roman state

and church, the attempt to establish the Monothelite doctrine as state orthodoxy led to a new controversy, While the Monophysites refused to accept it as an alternative to their belief in Christ's essentially divine nature, the Chalcedonian party rejected it not only because they considered it theologically unacceptable, but also on the grounds that it represented a cynical subjection of sacrosanct Christian doctrine to political expediency. Vehemently condemned by both sides, and failing to achieve its aim, the Monothelite doctrine was finally condemned in 680 as a pernicious heresy by the Sixth Council (the third council of Constantinople). By this time, the Monophysite churches (Coptic, Jacobite and Armenian), and also the Maronite church, had long fallen under Muslim rule and, like the Nestorian church before them (now also under Muslim rule), were no longer subject to Byzantine imperial sway (see Chapter 7).

5

The Iconoclast Controversy

The last major theological dispute to rock the ecumenical church (also, the last one to be settled by an ecumenical council) was the so-called iconoclast controversy (from the Greek *eikon,* 'image', combined with *klazein,* to 'break'). This controversy began in 726, when the Byzantine emperor Leo III (717–741) issued a decree banning the worship of 'icons', or sacred images, and their use in churches. (Icons were paintings of sacred subjects made on wood, their sanctity, and the miraculous powers attributed to particular icons, deriving from the belief that they were executed by monks under the influence of the Holy Spirit, after prolonged periods of prayer and fasting.) The proponents of iconoclasm saw in image worship a blatant breach of the second of the Ten Commandments ('Do not make for yourselves images of anything in heaven or on earth or in the water under the earth. Do not bow down to any idol or worship it, because I am the Lord your God and I tolerate no rivals . . .', Exodus 20.4–5). Behind the imperial policy of iconoclasm, however, historians have detected an attempt by the Byzantine emperors and church establishment to curb the growing social power and political influence of the monks.

One must stop here to explain that the development of Christian monasticism (from the Greek *monazein,* 'be alone') was independent from that of the church. It began from very early times with the ascetic practices of spiritually sensitive individuals who retired from the world to lead lives of religious contemplation as hermits, committing themselves to chastity (i.e. sexual abstinence) and the abandonment of worldly riches. A number of these hermits gained the reputation of being saints, their exemplary way of life setting a pattern for other sensitive individuals to follow. By the fourth century, a number of 'monastic' foundations were already established, in which a number of hermits or 'monks' led a 'common life' (the original Greek for a 'monastery' was *koinonion,* meaning a 'living together').

These early monastic foundations were not religious orders of the sort that was to emerge in Western Christendom later on. They had no set rules, and the relationship between them and the church remained undefined. The monks, moreover, had no clerical status unless they happened to be ordained clergymen, which was not ordinarily the case. Committed to perpetual self-denial, however, the monks gained the admiration and affection of ordinary Christian folk far more readily than the ordained clergy who wielded ecclesiastical authority but did not always lead exemplary lives. Consequently, the relations of the Christian laity with the monks tended to be far more intimate than their relations with the established church hierarchy. And it was as a result of this that monastic foundations came to acquire great social power with time; add to this the wealth accruing to many monasteries from pious donations of land, money or treasure. Icons made by the monks could be acquired from a monastery, normally in return for a small donation.

By the eighth century, the growth of monastic power in the Byzantine empire was beginning to alarm the ruling authorities, the state and established church alike. Monastic estates could not be taxed; and the more land was alienated to the monasteries, the more the Byzantine treasury suffered from such alienation. For a young man, moreover, joining a monastic order was the ideal way to avoid military service, at a time when Byzantium was locked in war with enemies on all sides, particularly with a Muslim caliphate at the peak of its conquering power in Damascus, then Baghdad. A monastery could also provide secure refuge for outlaws, or for people seeking immunity from prosecution by the state for whatever reason. And many monasteries probably did provide refuge for such elements. Most important of all, the monks by that time had acquired far more social power than the ruling establishment was willing to tolerate. Yet it was unthinkable for the state to curb the power of the monks by force without adequate religious justification. And the issue of icon worship, as a clear breach of the Second Commandment, appeared to Leo III and his 'iconoclast' successors to provide ample justification for the purpose.

The iconoclast movement in the history of Byzantium passed through two stages, the first lasting from 726 until 787, and the second from 817 until 843. During the first stage, resistance to the iconoclast policy of the emperors was strong but disorganized, with the army and administrative bureaucracy standing solidly on the side of the emperors, and resistance coming mainly from a strong body of 'iconodule' popular opinion backed by the writings of theologians such as John of Damascus. (This John of Damascus wrote in defence of image worship from the safety of his native city, then the capital of the Umayyad caliphate.) The second council of Nicaea (the Seventh Council, 787) brought this first stage of the iconoclast movement to an end by pronouncing image worship to be an essential part of Christian orthodoxy. During the second stage of the movement the monks, led by Theodore, abbot of the monastery of Stoudion in Constantinople, were better organized for resistance, which compelled the state to use force against them by organizing attacks on the more recalcitrant monasteries. In the more violent attacks some monks were killed, while others were seized, to be imprisoned or banished. But popular opinion remained generally on the side of the monks. Moreover, the state this time pursued its iconoclast policy at a disadvantage, as an ecumenical council had already ruled that image worship formed part of orthodoxy. To end the second stage of the controversy, no church council was needed, but simply a restoration of Orthodoxy: a ceremonial mass in the church of Saint Sophia in Constantinople, inaugurated by a solemn procession carrying back to the church the icons of which it had been divested, the dowager empress Theodora[1] leading the procession in person.

Thus the controversy ended, theologically, with a distinct triumph for the monks. But this triumph did not go beyond the limits of the theological. The emperors emerged from the controversy with their control of the state and the Byzantine see enhanced rather than diminished. The monks thereafter kept to their monasteries and abstained from interference in public affairs.

1. The effective ruler of the Byzantine empire from 842 until 856, Theodora, as the widow of the emperor Theophilus (829–842), was the leading figure in the council of regency for her son Michael III (842–867), who succeeded his father to the throne as a child.

6

The Schism between Rome and Constantinople

In the course of the iconoclast controversy, the church of Rome stood solidly on the side of image worship; and at the height of the controversy, the relations between the papacy and the church of Constantinople were strained almost to breaking point. Other factors, however, had long been causing tension between the two sides. In Constantinople, the church tended from the very beginning to be subservient to the emperors, who acquired with time the decisive say in the appointment of the patriarchs. The Roman popes, by contrast, originally elected by the people of Rome, ruled their church independently. Moreover, following the collapse of the Roman empire in the West (476) under the impact of repeated Germanic invasions, the political confusion that came to prevail in the lands under the jurisdiction of the Roman prelates left the papacy, for a long time, as the only institution qualified to serve as a unifying agent in these lands. In the enjoyment of the unrivalled authority which they acquired in consequence in the vast territory forming their see, the Roman popes, who had never deferred to imperial authority during the period when there was a separate line of emperors in Rome (395–476), were naturally less prepared to accept imperial directives from Constantinople. And before long, the Roman pontiffs began openly to defy the claim of the Byzantine emperors to political authority over all Christendom by crowning emperors in the West (Charlemagne in 800, Otto the Great in 962, historically recognized as the first ruler of what later came to be called the Holy Roman Empire). (This Western imperial institution continued until 1806, long after its emperors had ceased to be crowned by the popes.)

The difference in language between the Latin of the Roman church and the Greek of the Byzantine church did not help to smooth the relations between them. Nor did the old-attested ethnic prejudice between the Greeks and the Latins, whereby each side regarded the other as being insufferable on some score. All this considered, what is surprising is not that the two sides ultimately reached a parting of ways, but that they somehow managed to stay together for as long as they did. What kept them together, until the mid-eleventh century, was the principle of the unity of Christ's church on earth, to which both sides subscribed. Doctrinally, the two churches accepted the same orthodoxy, as defined by the seven ecumenical councils, the only bone of theological contention between them being the *Filioque* clause, which features in the Latin but not in the Greek version of the Nicene Creed (see Chapter 2). Whenever Greeks and Latins came to a quarrel, great issue was made of this *Filioque* clause, to cover up the more mundane reasons for the quarrel.

This was what happened in 867, the year of the so-called 'Photian Schism'. Nine years earlier, the Byzantine emperor Michael III (842–867) had removed a certain

Ignatius from the see of Constantinople and sent him into exile, to replace him as patriarch by the head of the imperial chancery, a learned layman called Photius. (Being no cleric, Photius had to be ordained deacon, then priest, then bishop in one ceremony, so he could qualify for consecration as patriarch.) In that same year, Nicholas I (858–867) became pope in Rome, and the supporters of Ignatius persuaded Pope Nicholas not to recognize the consecration of Photius. Rome, at the time, was angered by the missionary activity of Constantinople among the Bulgars, whom it claimed for its own sphere of jurisdiction; and Pope Nicholas, apart from not recognizing Photius, proceeded to write to the Bulgars and warn them against accepting the Greek preaching. In reaction, Photius brought up the issue of the *Filioque* clause, accused the Roman church of heresy for having altered the Nicene Creed, and declared Pope Nicholas deposed (867).

In that same year, however, the Byzantine emperor Michael III was murdered and succeeded by Basil the Macedonian (Basil I, 867–886). Photius was thereupon removed from the Byzantine patriarchate, and in a friendly gesture towards the papacy, Ignatius was reinstated. Interpreting the reinstatement of Ignatius as a Byzantine retreat, the next Roman pope, Adrian II (867–872), proceeded not only to secure a condemnation of Photius by his own church, but also to get the Greeks to submit to papal supremacy, which the Greeks were not prepared to do. Rather than making an issue of the matter, Basil I judiciously waited for Ignatius to die, whereupon he reappointed Photius to his place (877). The Muslims, by this time, were invading Sicily and southern Italy, and the Roman church, now in dire need of Byzantine military support, reluctantly agreed to recognize Photius. Thus, for the time being, a permanent schism (Latin *schisma,* from the Greek *schizein,* to 'split') between Rome and Constantinople was avoided, and the issue of the *Filioque* clause was politely dropped by the Greek side.

What followed in the West, in the course of the tenth century, was the Cluniac movement of spiritual revival, so called after the Benedictine monastery of Cluny, in the Rhone valley. (The Benedictine monastic order was established by Benedict of Nursia, died c.547; and its monastery at Cluny, which initiated the spiritual movement bearing its name, was founded in 909.) By the mid-eleventh century, the reformist spirit of this movement was being reflected in a reorganization of the Roman church, tightening its discipline to the considerable enhancement of papal power. And it was in the flush of its enhanced power that the papacy clashed once again with the Byzantine church, this time over the question of southern Italy.

Along with Sicily, southern Italy, with its considerable Greek population, was claimed as part of the Byzantine empire, and therefore as part of the diocese of Constantinople. By the mid-eleventh century, however, this Italian territory had fallen under the control of the Normans, who were Roman Catholics, and the popes found natural supporters in them against the Byzantine claim to southern Italy. Consequently, the Roman see, then under the reforming Pope Leo IX (1040–1054), began to impose the Latin church discipline on the local Greeks. The patriarch of Constantinople, Michael Kerullarius (1043–1059), retaliated by closing the Latin churches in Constantinople. When the Roman protests against the action taken by Kerullarius were ignored, the pope picked on three minor doctrinal and ecclesiastical issues (the absence of the *Filioque* clause from the Greek version of the Nicene Creed; the marriage of Greek priests; the Greek use of leavened bread for the eucharist) to pronounce the Byzantine patriarch and his church excommunicate by a formal 'bull', or papal letter (16 July 1054).

Treated at the time as a quarrel of ephemeral consequence within the Christian family, in which both sides were equally in the wrong, the schism of 1054 was followed by an estrangement between the churches of Rome and Constantinople which made the separation between them a permanent one. What this schism left behind was a Roman Catholic church in the West, and a Greek Orthodox church in the East, the latter followed by the Melchite communions of Antioch, Jerusalem and Alexandria.

7

The Difference Islam Made

By the time the churches of Constantinople and Rome had reached this parting of ways, the Christians of Egypt, Syria and Iraq had already been under Muslim rule for over four centuries. Among these Christians, the Melchites of the dioceses of Alexandria, Jerusalem and Antioch remained loyal to Byzantium, as they had been before. The Nestorians and the Monophysites, on the other hand, having always regarded Byzantium as a political and ecclesiastical oppressor, had perceived Muslim rule from the very start as a welcome relief from Byzantine oppression. The same, apparently, was true of the Maronites, especially after 680 – the year in which the Sixth Council condemned the Monothelite confession as a wicked heresy. Hence the readiness with which the Nestorians and the Monophysites – and perhaps also the Maronites, but not the Melchites – co-operated with Muslim political authority.

Because of their known loyalty to Byzantium, the Melchites of the Muslim Arab empire were the Christian communion that was least favoured. In Syria as in Egypt, they had originally comprised two different ethnic elements, one Greek, the other native. When Syria and Egypt were conquered by the Muslim Arabs, most of the

Greeks left, the remaining ones merging with the native Syrian or Egyptian population in due course. In Syria, where the native Arameo-Arab element among the Melchites had always been substantial, perhaps to the extent of forming the majority, the Melchite community survived in force, in the diocese of Antioch as in that of Jerusalem. In the diocese of Alexandria, however, where the overwhelming majority of the native Coptic population followed the Monophysite Coptic church, the Melchites survived only as a small minority composed of Egyptianized Greeks and Hellenized Copts.

The Egyptian Melchite church thus emerged in the wake of the Arab conquests considerably weakened. The Melchite patriarch of Alexandria fled the city when it was captured by the Muslims. In 642, his flight made it possible for the patriarch of the Coptic communion to re-establish himself in the city after whose name his see was actually called. Shortly after, the Melchite see was also re-established in Alexandria. For a period of seventy-five years, however, it had no occupants (652–727). Once the Alexandrian Melchite church came to have its patriarchs again, these patriarchs tended to be subservient to Constantinople. Yet they remained sufficiently conscious of the antiquity and eminence of their independent apostolic status not to follow the lead of Constantinople unquestioningly on all issues. Thus, when the schism between Constantinople and Rome took place in 1054, the Melchite patriarchs of Alexandria only agreed to take the Byzantine side in the schism after prolonged reluctance.

In the see of Jerusalem, the Christians, who appear to have been solidly Melchite, had been judicious enough to surrender to the Muslim Arabs on favourable terms at the time of the conquest (638). Consequently, Melchite patriarchs continued to succeed one another to that see on a regular basis until the fall of Jerusalem to the Crusaders (1099), the Muslim authorities leaving them to manage their church affairs as they pleased.

The situation was somewhat different with respect to the Melchite see of Antioch. Once the Muslim Arab conquest of Syria was completed (641), the city of Antioch became one of the principal *'awasim*, or strategic outposts, forming the Muslim line of defence against the Byzantines in Anatolia. And certainly at the initial stages, the continuing presence of a pro-Byzantine Christian patriarchate in a Muslim outpost of such strategic importance was unacceptable. Hence, until the end of the seventh century, the Melchite see of Antioch could only have titular patriarchs resident in Constantinople. Later, when the Melchite patriarchate was re-established in Antioch in 702, it remained unrecognized by the Muslim Arabs for forty years, and barely recognized thereafter.

In 969, however, the Byzantines managed to recapture Antioch from the Muslims, after which they succeeded in extending their Syrian reconquests to include most of the valley of the Orontes river (what the ancient Greeks called *Koilosyria*, or 'Hollow Syria'). With the city of Antioch once more in Byzantine hands (969–1085), its Melchite see became fully subservient to Constantinople. And as the churches of Constantinople and Rome broke relations with one another at a time when the Byzantines were in complete control of Antioch, it was only natural that the Antiochene Melchite see should have followed Constantinople in the schism. The see of Jerusalem, which had consistently followed the ecclesiastical lead of Constantinople, was also quick to do so. Originally, the Melchites of the see of Jerusalem had followed a Jerusalemite Syriac rite of their own, while those of the see of Alexandria had followed an Alexandrian Coptic rite, and those of Antioch an Antiochene Syriac rite. Or at least so it is believed. In time, however, as circumstances forced the Melchites everywhere to become increasingly dependent on Byzantium, they abandoned their original ethnic rites, probably by stages, to adopt in their place the Greek rite of the Byzantine church.

It was in the last decades of the seventh century, when the titular holders of the Melchite see of Antioch were still residing in Constantinople, that the Maronites began to elect patriarchs of their own to that see. Maronite tradition maintains that the first of these patriarchs was John Marun, abbot of the monastic foundation of Dayr Marun, in the Orontes valley (see Chapter 4); also, that this John Marun was elected to the Antiochene see in 680, immediately following the condemnation of the Mono-thelite doctrine as a heresy by the Sixth Council. According to the same Maronite tradition, it was Patriarch John Marun who first moved the seat of the Maronite patriarchate from Dayr Marun to the village of Kafarhayy, in the northern reaches of Mount Lebanon, because of the violent persecution suffered by his church and community at the hands of the Byzantines in the Orontes valley. The Byzantines could not have persecuted the Maronites in Syria at a time when they had no political, military or ecclesiastical presence in the country. They could easily have carried out such a persecution, however, during the period between the tenth and eleventh centuries, following their reconquest of Antioch and the Orontes valley (see above). Muslim Arab records of the first half of the tenth century indicate that the Orontes valley during that period was still the home of the Maronites. By the end of the eleventh century, however, that same valley had come to be inhabited by Melchites, no doubt as a result of the Byzantine reoccupation of the area between 969 and 1085. Meanwhile, the Maronites had come to be established in force in Mount Lebanon, except for a Maronite enclave in and around Aleppo. This was the only city of northern Syria which remained in Muslim hands, the Byzantines never having been successful in their attempts to recapture it.

It is hardly imaginable that the Maronites would have initially succeeded in breaking away from the Byzantine communion as easily as they did, had Syria been still under Byzantine rule in 680. And it is possible that the Maronite church would not have survived the Byzantine reconquests in Syria between the tenth and eleventh centuries, and maintained itself as a Christian communion on its own, had the Byzantines at the time succeeded in occupying the whole of Syria, leaving no parts under Muslim rule where dissident Christian groups could find refuge from Byzantine persecution.

It has been argued that the Monophysite and Nestorian communions might not have managed to retain their ecclesiastical independence any more than the Maronites, had the Byzantines in the seventh century succeeded in preventing the Muslim Arab takeover of Egypt, Syria and Iraq. To the Copts in Egypt, as to the Jacobites in Syria and the Nestorians in Iraq, the Muslim conquests of that period as already noted appeared in their time as a deliverance from Byzantine oppression, no matter what the cost of this deliverance was to the broader cause of Christendom. Wherever they happened to be found, the Monophysites and Nestorians, unlike the Melchites. were quick to take the side of the Muslim conquerors and co-operate with them, to the extreme embarrassment of Byzantium. In Syria and Iraq, where the Christian population was largely (and perhaps predominantly) Arab, the Muslim conquerors were apparently perceived (and in many cases openly welcomed) as fellow Arabs rather than as aliens, such as the Greeks and Romans had been to them. And certainly at the initial stage, the Muslims did not attempt to impose their religion on the Arab and Aramaeo-Arab Christian populations that came under their rule. In accordance with Qur'anic authority, Islam classified all Christians (and also all Jews) living under its dominance as *ahl kitab*: 'scriptural communities' entitled to the free exercise of their religion under the Muslim *dhimmah,* or protection of conscience. What was expected from such *dhimmah* communities in return was that they should abide by the Muslim political order and pay a special poll tax, called the *jizyah*. (Muslim jurisprudence was later to transform these simple Qur'anic precepts regarding the tolerance of *dhimmah* communities into a set of socially restrictive and discriminatory regulations, though few of them were regularly applied as articulated.)

What Islam actually guaranteed for the Nestorian, Monophysite and Monothelite Christians of its empire was protection against unsolicited external interventions in their affairs, which could have otherwise compromised – or perhaps terminated – their existence as independent

communions. Of these three communions, the Monophysite was the largest.

In Egypt, where the Monophysite Copts represented the
vast majority of the native population, the Arab conquest
not only made it possible for the Coptic patriarchs to
return to Alexandria (as already observed), but also consecrated the ascendancy of the Coptic over the Melchite
communion in the country. The Coptic patriarchs continued to reside in Alexandria for as long as Egypt
remained a province of the Umayyad caliphate of
Damascus (661–750), then of the Abbassid caliphate of
Baghdad (750–1258), administered by Umayyad or
Abbassid governors residing in the city of al-Fustat, at the
apex of the Nile Delta. Meanwhile, in 909 a rival caliphate
was established by the dynasty of the Fatimids in
al-Mahdiyya (today in Tunisia): and in 969, the Fatimids
conquered Egypt, then proceeded to move the seat of their
caliphate to Cairo (973), a new capital which they had
specially built for themselves outside al-Fustat. Thereupon,
practical considerations made it necessary for the Coptic
patriarchs to move their residence to Cairo (actually, to
al-Fustat, now a suburb of the new Cairo). Here, the
leadership of the Coptic communion could be closer to the
central Muslim authority: also, the Muslim government
could keep the Coptic church under closer watch: a matter
of prime importance, considering that the Copts continued
to form a major part (by some historical estimates, the
majority) of the Egyptian population until the twelfth
century.

In Syria, where the Melchite communion, with its strong
pro-Byzantine sympathies, retained a much larger following than it did in Egypt, the Muslims had special reason to

favour the Syrian Monophysite communion of the Jacobites against them. And what probably made the Muslim Arab attitude towards the Syrian Jacobites more openly positive than it was towards the Egyptian Copts was the fact that the Syrian Jacobites – like the Syrian Melchites and Maronites – were by their majority Arab or Aramaeo-Arab, while the Copts in Egypt remained conscious of their separate historical ethnicity and for a time even kept their Coptic language, continuing to speak it among themselves.

The fact that so many Jacobites in Syria were not only staunchly anti-Byzantine, but also ethnically Arab, appears to have had two effects. On the one hand, it made the Muslim Arabs feel a special affinity towards them. On the other, it inclined the Jacobites to co-operate with Muslim Arab rule in a special way. From an early time, the community placed its considerable resources at the service of the emerging Muslim Arab civilization. Learned Jacobites speaking Arabic, and at the same time knowledgeable in Syriac (the language of their liturgy) and often also in Greek, played the leading role in translating the classics of Greek science and philosophy into Arabic, frequently through the intermediary of Syriac. By so doing, they laid the foundations for the Muslim achievements in these fields.

Though styled patriarchs of Antioch, the heads of the Jacobite church do not appear to have actually established a recognized residence for themselves in that city at any time. Their residence, rather, shifted from place to place according to convenience. In Islamic times, it came to be fixed at some stage at Melitene (modern Malatiya, north of Aleppo, and today in Turkey). By the eleventh century, however, the Byzantine reoccupation of northern Syria was making the continuing stay of the Jacobite patriarchs at Melitene extremely difficult. This made them abandon the place in 1031, to establish a new residence for themselves in or around Amida (modern Diyarbekir, in eastern Turkey): a city on the east bank of the Tigris, well within the Muslim territory of northern Mesopotamia. By the seventeenth century, their seat had come to be fixed outside Amida, in the monastery of Dayr al-Za'faran, near the town of Mardin.

The Nestorians in Iraq, like the Jacobites in Syria, welcomed the Muslim Arab conquest of their country and co-operated with Muslim rule. They also contributed to the development of Muslim science and thought, as the Jacobites did, by their activity in translating Greek texts into Arabic, their contribution to Islamic science being particularly important in the field of medicine. When the Abbassids moved the seat of the Muslim caliphate from Syria to Iraq (750), then established their capital at Baghdad (762), not far north of the old Persian capital of Seleucia-Ctesiphon, the catholicoi of the Nestorian church were quick to move their residence to the new Muslim capital, where they could be close to the caliphs and enjoy their favour. The Nestorian church continued to flourish in Baghdad until the city fell to the Mongols in 1258, whereupon the seat of its catholicoi was moved to the vicinity of Mosul and Alqosh, in northern Iraq.

The coming of Islam, however, did have an adverse effect on Nestorian missionary activity in Central Asia, and also on Jacobite and Nestorian missionary activity in India and East Africa. This activity, in its time, had been connected with the trade between the Byzantine and

Persian empires and the lands of the Indian Ocean basin and the Far East, and had actually followed the routes of that trade. It was only natural, therefore, that it should have declined as this trade began to pass into Muslim hands, and that it should have ceased altogether as the same trade turned into a Muslim monopoly.

Another adverse effect which Islam had on both the Nestorian and the Jacobite communions was the depletion of their numbers through large-scale conversion. Before Islam, the Nestorians had been essentially a Persian church, its followers counting not only Mesopotamian Arabs and Aramaeo-Arabs, but also large numbers of Persians. And the rapid and massive conversion of the Persians of the former Sassanid territories to Islam, following the completion of the Muslim conquest of these territories in 651, must have taken the first heavy toll of the Nestorian church adherents. Next followed the conversion of most of the Christian Arab tribes (as distinct from the rural and urban Arabs and Aramaeo-Arabs) to Islam, in Syria as in Mesopotamia: conversions that involved whole groups rather than individuals. Most notable was the conversion of the Syro-Mesopotamian tribe of the Taghlib, which appears to have been completed by the early tenth century, at which time the Taghlib tribal bishopric passed out of existence. Before their conversion, the Taghlib Arabs used to follow the Jacobite rite and revere St Sergius as their special patron. As they, and other Arab tribes, turned Muslim, the Christian communions to which they had formerly belonged – mainly, the Jacobite and the Nestorian – were left with followings whose speech, for the most part, was Syriac rather than Arabic. Thus, paradoxically, the Syrian and Mesopotamian Christian communions originally most favoured by the Muslim Arabs, and most favourably disposed towards them, were the ones least able to retain the original Arab side to their character.

The Melchites, by contrast, did retain their Arab ethnicity under Islam, although their strong allegiance to Byzantium deterred them from cooperating with Muslim rule in the manner of the Jacobites and Nestorians. The same was true of the Maronites, whose ethnic character remained distinctly Arab, even though they, like the Jacobites and Nestorians, retained Syriac as the language of their liturgy.

8

The Maronite Union with Rome

The twelfth and thirteenth centuries in the lands of the Near East were the period of the crusades (1096–1291), during which 'Frankish' (i.e. West European) armies carrying the banner of the Roman popes conquered the greater part of Syria from the Muslims, organizing their conquests in four 'Latin' (i.e. Roman Catholic) states: the Principality of Antioch (1098–1268), the County of Edessa (1098–1146), the Kingdom of Jerusalem (1099–1291), and the County of Tripoli (1109–1289). Among the Christians of Syria, the chief sufferers from the crusades were the Melchites, the Syrian followers of Byzantine orthodoxy whose schism with Rome was still a live issue at the time of the first crusade, being then barely fifty years old. In Antioch, as in Jerusalem, the crusaders were quick to secure the election of Latin prelates to the Melchite apostolic sees. As for the Melchite occupants of these sees, they were forced to flee for refuge to Constantinople, where they and their titular successors were to remain until the Muslim reconquest of the holy lands was completed. Because the Mamluk reconquest of Antioch, in 1268, left the city in ruins, reducing it to little more than a village, the returning Melchite patriarchs had to take up residence elsewhere, ultimately establishing themselves in Damascus, the capital of the largest of the Mamluk provinces – and later, of the Ottoman provinces – of Syria. Damascus appears to have become the permanent seat of these patriarchs in 1375, or shortly after.

Where the non-Melchite Christians of Syria were concerned, it was a different matter. The crusaders had hardly established themselves in the country when the Latin church, from the vantage of Antioch and Jerusalem, set out to develop relations with these non-Melchites. The rejection of ecumenical orthodoxy by these communions had emanated, historically, from hostile sentiments directed more against nearby Byzantium than against distant Rome, which made them amenable to Roman overtures. Among the groups in question, the most important to the crusaders were the Armenians, followed by the Maronites, both of them warlike peoples who willingly placed their military resources at the disposal of the crusader cause. By the time of the first crusade, colonies of Armenians were already established among the Syrian Jacobites and Nestorians in the territory of Edessa (modern Urfa, in Turkey), in the Euphrates country close by the Anatolian border; also among the Syrian Melchites and Jacobites in the territory of Cilicia, around the Gulf of Alexandretta, which came in time to be called Lesser Armenia (as distinct from the Greater Armenia in eastern Asia Minor). The Byzantines had encouraged the migration of the Armenians to these Anatolian borderlands since the tenth century, to help garrison their lines of defence against the Muslim lands to the south. When the crusaders arrived in Antioch, the local Armenians assisted them in the capture of the city, as they assisted them also in the capture of Edessa. The crusaders consequently came to hold them in the highest esteem.

The Maronites, for their part, were already established in the northern mountain reaches of the Lebanon by the time of the crusades. As the crusader armies, following the capture of Antioch, proceeded southwards in 1099 along the Syrian coast, in the direction of Jerusalem, they stopped to celebrate Easter outside Tripoli, where bands of Maronites descended from their mountains to meet them and offer them their services as auxiliaries and guides. Later, when Tripoli was captured, and the County of Tripoli was established to include the northern parts of the Lebanon, a number of Maronite chieftains placed themselves and their men at the service of the counts of Tripoli and their Frankish vassals. The fact that other Maronites rejected Frankish rule and occasionally rose in arms against it did not detract from the positive attitude which the Franks retained towards the community as a body.

Roman Catholic efforts to attract such friendly Eastern Christians to the Latin fold were exerted mainly from Antioch, where the Latin church appears to have been particularly active. And positive results did not take long to be achieved. Among the Syrian-speaking Jacobites and Nestorians of northern Syria and Mesopotamia, a number (including some leading clerics) were willing to convert to Roman orthodoxy and declare allegiance to the Roman popes. But the greater success of the Latins was among the Armenians of northern Syria and Cilicia. By the fourth decade of the twelfth century, the Armenian church, under its supreme catholicos, had entered into formal communion with the papacy.

The same was to happen in the case of the Maronites, whose contacts with the popes of Rome, reportedly, were initiated by the Maronite patriarchate as early as 1100.

Overtures for a Maronite union with the Roman church followed, one of them in connection with the negotiations which led to the Armenian conversion. According to the crusader historian William of Tyre (d. 1185), however, the Maronites only agreed to abjure the Monothelite confession and enter into union with Rome in c.1180. What is historically certain is that one of their patriarchs, Jeremiah of 'Amshit (died 1230), attended the opening sessions of the Lateran Council held in Rome in 1216, in response to an official invitation extended to him by Pope Innocent III (1198–1216).

Once the last crusaders had left Syria, the union between the Armenian church and Rome became casual, finally lapsing in 1345 without a formal schism. Also, by then, the sporadic Jacobite and Nestorian flirtations with the papacy, which may never have been of particularly serious moment, had abated. The Maronite church, however, never officially abandoned its union with the Roman church, despite much initial opposition to this union in the ranks of the Maronite lower clergy and laity; and also, despite the difficulties involved in maintaining communications with the Roman popes on a regular basis after the Mamluk sultans of Egypt had expelled the last crusaders from the Syrian coast in 1291.

During the period when Syria was wholly under Mamluk rule, the Maronite patriarchs remained in touch with Rome on an intermittent basis through the intermediary of the Franciscan *Fratres Minori* (or Lesser Brothers), whose order, founded by Saint Francis of Assisi in 1209, established its *Terra Santa* (or Holy Land) mission in Jerusalem with Mamluk permission in 1291, also maintaining a branch in Beirut. In 1439, when Pope Eugene IV invited the patriarch of Constantinople, along with other Eastern Christian prelates, to a special council in the city of Florence to consider the termination of the schism between the Eastern churches and Rome, the Maronite patriarch John of Jaj, unable to travel to Italy in person, delegated the abbot of the Franciscans of Beirut to represent him at that council. The delegate was instructed to inform the pope of the patriarch's unconditional submission to papal authority, and of the continuing and unwavering loyalty of the Maronite church and community to the Roman see.

As far as it can be known, the popes of Rome, until that time, had never addressed the heads of the Maronite church as patriarchs of the apostolic see of Antioch. The papacy continued to reserve this title for the Melchite holders of that see for as long as the popes still hoped for an end to the schism with the Eastern churches. From the point of view of Rome, moreover, the Melchites of the apostolic sees of Antioch and Jerusalem were schismatics, not heretics. This made the ordination of their clergy ecumenically valid, and in keeping with the principle of apostolic succession. Not so the ordination of the clergy in communions classified as being of heterodox origin, such as the Maronites, whose original Monothelite confession was considered to have placed their clergy – patriarchs and all – outside the pale of the apostolic tradition. To remedy the historical break in this tradition, and transform the Maronite church – now united with Rome – into an apostolic communion with a clergy whose ecclesiastical status was ecumenically valid, its patriarchs, once elected, had to be confirmed in office by the popes, and so receive their apostolic authority from the see of Rome.

When the Council of Florence failed to put an end to the

schism between Rome and Byzantium, the Roman church apparently ceased to be much concerned about reserving the title of patriarch of Antioch for the Melchite holder of that see. By 1456 the Maronite patriarch was already being addressed by that title, although his apostolic authority, though titularly related to Antioch, was to continue to depend on papal confirmation, and so derive from Rome.

Meanwhile, following the Council of Florence, the relations between the Maronite church and Rome became more regular. Between 1450 and 1475, a Franciscan monk, *Fra* Gryphon (or Brother Gryphon) of Flanders, was detailed to the monastery of Qannubin, the seat of the Maronite patriarchs, to serve as Roman Catholic adviser to the Maronite church. This Fra Gryphon inducted three young Maronites into the Franciscan order in 1470, arranging for them to travel to Italy to study. One of them, Gabriel Ibn al-Qila'i (died 1516), returned from Italy in 1493 to become the first native Roman Catholic adviser to the Maronite patriarch, and missionary to his own people.

What followed in Western Europe was the Protestant Reformation, then the Roman Catholic Reformation. And in connection with the latter movement came a new surge of Roman Catholic missionary activity in the world, in which the leading role was played by the emerging order of the Jesuit Fathers (the Society of Jesus, founded by St Ignatius Loyola in 1534); also, by the Capuchins (full name, Order of the Friars Minor Capuchin). These were a branch of the Franciscan order formed in 1529, and devoted to missionary work and preaching. In Syria, by now under Ottoman rule (1516–1918), the Jesuits and Capuchins rapidly replaced the Franciscans as the principal Roman Catholic missionaries, and also as the

chief intermediaries between the Maronite church and
Rome. In 1596, one Jesuit father, Jerome Dandidi, was
sent from Rome to convene a synod of the Maronite
church at Qannubin, the mountain seat of the Maronite
patriarchs, with a view to introducing ecclesiastical
reforms in keeping with Roman Catholic practice. A little
over a decade earlier, in 1585, Pope Gregory XIII (1572–
1585) had founded a special seminary in Rome (the
Collegium Maronitarum) for the education and training of
young Maronites aspiring for church office; and in 1608, a
graduate of that seminary, John Makhluf, was elected
Maronite patriarch. Another graduate of Rome to succeed
to the leadership of the Maronite church was Patriarch
Stephen al-Duwayhi (1668–1704), a man of great learning
and a distinguished historian, in whose time the first
Maronite monastic order was founded. In 1736, a second
Maronite synod, held in the monastery of Dayr al-
Luwayzah, revised and continued the work of the earlier
synod of Qannubin, completing the transformation of the
Maronite church into a communion fully united with
Rome, yet retaining its traditional clerical structure and
discipline within the union, along with its special
Antiochene Syriac rite.

9

The Emergence of the Uniate Churches

From the time the Maronite union with Rome went into effect in the course of the twelfth century, it continued without interruption, providing an example which other Christians of the Near Eastern lands were to follow in due course, non-Melchites and Melchites alike. And why this was so deserves some explanation. For the duration of the Mamluk period (1250–1517), the Mamluk sultans of Cairo, like all Muslim sultans and caliphs before them, had guaranteed freedom of worship for their non-Muslim subjects, granting the different Christian and Jewish sects under their rule individual recognition and, by and large, equal treatment. Under the Ottomans, however, who succeeded the Mamluks in the rule of the Arab lands (1516–1918), the non-Muslim subjects of the sultans of Istanbul came to be classified in three categories, and initially no more. The Jews, along with the remnants of the Samaritan sect in Palestine, were classified as the *Millet-i Yahud,* or Jewish community, the management of their religious and other special affairs entrusted to the grand rabbi of Istanbul. As for the Christians, they were arbitrarily classified until the mid-nineteenth century in only two categories: those of Greek rite, called the *Millet-i Rum,* or Greek community; and those of non-Greek rite, collectively viewed as forming the *Millet-i Arman,* or Armenian community. Thus the *Millet-i Arman* included not only the Armenians of the Gregorian communion, but also the communions of Syriac rite, notably the Jacobites, the Nestorians and the Maronites.

This *Millet* system (as historians have called it) produced grave disaffections and dissatisfactions within the ranks of the Christians of the empire. While the Maronites, firmly united with Rome and protected by Roman Catholic European powers, were not much bothered by their Ottoman classification as part of the *Millet-i Arman,* the Jacobites and the Nestorians resented their official inclusion in a *Millet* to which they were ethnically alien (and, in the case of the Nestorians, also doctrinally alien). To Jacobites and Nestorians who felt like this, Catholic missionaries readily offered a solution: ignore the *Millet* system altogether, or at least gain immunity from it, by following the example of the Maronites and entering into union with powerful Rome.

Among the Christians of Greek rite, the *Millet* system was eminently suitable to the Greek followers of the see of Constantinople. But it was far from being as suitable to the Melchites of the sees of Antioch, Jerusalem and Alexandria. With a Greek of the Christian Phanar quarter of Istanbul (today called the Fener) heading the *Millet-i Rum,* it was only natural that most, if not all, of his subordinates – in the see of Constantinople, as in those of Antioch, Jerusalem and Alexandria – would be Greeks (and normally Phanariot Greeks) like himself. This meant that only the lower clergy – mainly the parish priests – in

Syria, Palestine and Egypt would be natives of their respective countries. By the late seventeenth century, many
Melchites in the countries in question were growing resent-
ful of the established Greek ecclesiastical dominance over
them. And to such Melchites, the Roman Catholic missionaries offered the easiest way out: ignore the *Millet* system and gain freedom from Phanariot Greek dominance,
again by following the example of the Maronites and unit-
ing with Rome.

Ever since they became active in the Near Eastern
countries, the different Roman Catholic missionary orders
had been establishing churches of Latin rite ministering
to Roman Catholic West European expatriates wherever
they happened to be found. And native Christians of
different denominations were attracted to attend the
Latin services in these churches, albeit in relatively
small numbers. Some of these became regular Roman
Catholics, locally called the 'Latins' *(al-Latin)*. Meanwhile,
under the influence of the Roman Catholic missionaries,
each of the various Eastern Christian communions split
between a Uniate and a non-Uniate branch, each branch
becoming a church independent of the other, the Uniate
one accepting and maintaining communion with the
Roman see.

Among the Melchites of the see of Antioch, the split
began in Aleppo, where Jesuit and Capuchin missionaries
had been active among the local Christian population since
1626, their activities also affecting the Christians of
Damascus. It was under their influence that a Damascene
Melchite cleric, Euthymius Sayfi (c.1648–1723), openly
declared his allegiance to Rome in 1683, after which he
proceeded to organize a Uniate monastic order under his

leadership: the Basilian order of the Congregation of Our Saviour (or Salvatorian order). Sayfi, at the time, was serving as Melchite bishop of Tyre (today in Lebanon), but he had many followers among the well-to-do Melchites of Aleppo and his native Damascus: Arab Melchites who had long been disgruntled by the Greek dominance over their church.

When the Melchite see of Antioch fell vacant in 1724, the year following Sayfi's death, his Uniate followers elected one of their own number, Cyril VI, as the new patriarch, while the opponents of this Cyril elected a non-Uniate candidate called Sylvester to the same post. Both patriarchs established themselves in Damascus. But the Ottoman government, prompted by the patriarch of Constantinople, accorded its recognition to Sylvester, although it was Cyril who had been elected first. With this disputed patriarchal election, the split in the Antiochene Melchite church between the 'Greek Catholic' followers of Euthymius, Sayfi and Cyril, and the 'Greek Orthodox' followers of Sylvester, became complete and permanent. Persecuted by the Greek Orthodox, who enjoyed the official Ottoman backing (the Ottoman government, it seems, did not recognize the existence of a *Millet-i Katolik* among its Christian subjects until 1839), the Greek Catholics began to migrate from Aleppo and other parts of the Syrian interior to Mount Lebanon, where the Maronites, as fellow Roman Catholics, were in a position to protect them and make them feel welcome. Meanwhile, some conversions to the Uniate cause began to occur among the Melchites of the sees of Jerusalem and Alexandria, but not to the extent of creating a split in either of these two sees. Consequently, the head of the

Uniate Melchite (or Greek Catholic) church in all three of these sees became one, styled patriarch of Antioch, Alexandria, Jerusalem and all the East. His permanent residence today is in the Lebanese capital, Beirut.

Shortly after the split between the Greek Catholic and Greek Orthodox branches of the Melchite communion became complete, a similar split took place within the Armenian communion. And as in the case of the Melchites, this split took place in Aleppo, where the Armenian bishop of the city, Abraham Artzivian, fell under the local Roman Catholic missionary influence and turned Catholic. When Artzivian, in 1740, was elected Armenian patriarch of Sis, in Cilicia, he effectively became the first head of the Uniate, Armenian Catholic (as distinct from the non-Uniate, Armenian Orthodox) church. Subsequently, the head of this Uniate communion came to be styled patriarch of the Catholic Armenians and catholicos of Cilicia. Like the Greek Catholics before them, the Armenian Catholics, persecuted by the Armenian Orthodox in their original homelands, migrated in large numbers to Mount Lebanon, to live among the Maronites. The residence of their catholicos was established in the village of Bzummar, in the Kisrawan mountains.

It was also in seventeenth-century Aleppo, under Jesuit and Capuchin influence, that the Jacobite communion began to divide between Uniate and non-Uniate branches. Two centuries earlier, one of three Jacobite patriarchs contending the see of Antioch, Bahnam al-Hadli, had sent an emissary called 'Abdallah of Edessa to Italy to represent him at the Council of Florence, and declare allegiance to

the Roman papacy on his behalf (1444). But the union thus
effected between one sector of the Jacobite church and
Rome was casual and short-lived. In 1656, however, a
Jacobite convert to Catholicism, Andrew Akhidjan, was
elected bishop of the Jacobite diocese of Aleppo; and this
same Akhidjan, in 1662, was elected patriarch of 'all
Syrians'. (It must be noted here that the Jacobites actually
called themselves *Suryan,* or Syrians.) What followed was
a period when the Syrian Catholics (as the followers of
Akhidjan were called) suffered persecution at the hands of
the non-Uniate Jacobites, or Syrian Orthodox, so that their
Uniate communion lost its cohesion for the duration of
almost a century. The Syrian Catholic church, however,
was reconstituted – this time more effectively, and on a
permanent basis – in 1782, when another Syrian Catholic
bishop of Aleppo, Michael Jarweb, was elected patriarch
of the Uniate Jacobites. Originally established in Dayr
al-Za'faran, near Mardin, in the Euphrates country, the
successors of Jarweh in the patriarchate of the Syrian
Catholic church subsequently moved to Dayr al-Sharfeh,
in the Kisrawan mountains of the Lebanon, which remains
their summer residence. Their permanent, winter residence
was later established in Beirut.

In Egypt, a Uniate Coptic communion first emerged in
1741, when a Coptic bishop called Athanasius abandoned
the Monophysite confession of his church and accepted
Roman orthodoxy. The Uniate Copts, however, never
large in number, were not organized as a church on
their own until 1895, when Pope Leo XIII divided
their small communion of 5,000 into three dioceses under
one administrator, subsequently styled patriarch of
Alexandria, but residing in Cairo. This communion came

to be called the Coptic Catholic church, to distinguish it from the Monophysite, Coptic Orthodox church.

Older than all these Uniate churches, except for the Maronite, was the Nestorian Catholic communion. Attending the Council of Florence, alongside the representative of the Jacobite patriarch Bahnam al-Hadli, were representatives of the Cyprus branch of the Nestorian church, whose principal base was still in Iraq. These Nestorians, like the Jacobite patriarch, were persuaded to adopt the Roman Catholic confession and declare allegiance to Roman papacy, whereupon they came to be called the Chaldaeans (as distinct from the Nestorians who refused to unite with Rome, and later began to call themselves Assyrians, and their church the Assyrian Orthodox church). Subsequently, in 1551, Pope Julius III appointed a leading Catholic Nestorian, John Sulaka, as first patriarch of his Uniate church. The successors of Sulaka later adopted the title of patriarch-catholicos of Babylon and the Chaldaeans. Significantly, the Chaldaean is the only Uniate church whose membership grew to exceed by far in numbers the membership of the communion from which it originally split.

10

The Arab Protestant Churches

Historically, the advent of Protestantism to the Arab world was a by-product of the movement of Protestant religious awakening of the eighteenth and early nineteenth centuries called Evangelicalism. This movement had first emerged in the United States and Britain, where it aimed to remedy the social evils resulting from the industrial revolution by a missionary activity emphasizing the absolute authority and reliability of the Bible, and the individual need for spiritual transformation through Bible reading, prayer, trust in Christ, and the modelling of the individual's life on the Gospels. The Evangelicals organized themselves in voluntary societies which printed and distributed the Bible and religious tracts, founded and ran Sunday schools, and established educational institutions of all levels, where Evangelical preaching formed an essential part of the curriculum. Rather than being limited to one Protestant denomination to the exclusion of others, the Evangelical movement was common to all, and co-operation between different Protestant denominations in Evangelical activity was more the rule than the exception. By the early nineteenth century, Evangelicalism finally went forth beyond its original home grounds, to become a full-scale Protestant missionary movement touching all parts of the world, among them the Near Eastern lands.

The Protestant Christian faith, from which the Evangelical missionary movement sprang, had its beginnings in the sixteenth century, when the first Protestant communions emerged in Germany and other parts of northern Europe, rejecting the authority of Rome. Essentially, Protestantism developed as a reaction to mediaeval Roman Catholic doctrines and practices which seemed difficult to justify in terms of the Bible, or which appeared to contradict the authority of the Bible. While the Protestant Christian confession differs in detail from one denomination to another, all Protestants hold the Bible to be the only basis of Christian religious authority, with which every Christian must be individually and directly familiar. Moreover, all Protestants maintain that human salvation is achieved not collectively, through participation in the sacraments administered by the church, but individually, and through faith. This fundamental Protestant precept depends on the authority of Paul ('For it is by God's grace you have been saved through faith. It is not the result of your own efforts, but God's gift, so that no one can boast about it', Ephesians 2.8–9; 'The person who is put right with God through faith shall live', Romans 1.17). All Protestants, moreover, confess the priesthood of all believers, regarding their churchmen as 'ministers' or 'pastors' charged with the leadership of church services, and attendance to the spiritual needs of their congregations, without wielding actual priestly authority. Ecclesiastically, some Protestant denominations, such as the Anglicans (or Episcopalians), maintain the clerical hierarchy of deacons, priests and bishops for their church, without attributing any truly sacerdotal authority to them. Other denominations have different arrangements. The Presbyterians, for example, replace the traditional ecclesiastical hierarchy in their communion with a collegiate sort of church government composed of pastors and lay leaders, the latter called 'elders' or 'presbyters' (hence the name of the denomination). While the Presbyterian communion in any given country or area maintains a central administration, or synod, providing co-ordination between its different presbyteries, the Congregationalists, though hardly differing from the Presbyterians in doctrinal confession, maintain the right and duty of each congregation (i.e. each individual presbytery, or church unit) to take its own decisions and run its own affairs, independently of any superior or co-ordinating authority. In the Society of Friends, or Quakers, the principle of the priesthood of all believers is taken to its logical extreme. The Quakers have no ordained ministers of any kind, and come together for informal community prayer as spiritual equals not in churches, but in what they call meeting houses.

Protestant preaching activity started in Ottoman Syria in the early 1820s, with the arrival of the first Presbyterian and Congregational Evangelical missionaries in Beirut. By the 1840s, these missionaries, operating in Beirut and the Druze parts of Mount Lebanon, had already established their first schools and seminaries for the local Christians, winning the first converts among them. Meanwhile, beginning from that same period, British missionaries – Anglicans in Palestine and Transjordan, representatives of the Scottish Presbyterian and British Reformed churches in Mount Lebanon and the Syrian interior – began to make their appearance on the scene. And starting in 1860, the first German Lutheran missionaries arrived in Palestine from Prussia. The efforts of these German missionaries resulted in the emergence of a small Lutheran Arab community which survives to the present day in Jordan and Palestine/Israel.

The vehicle for Anglican missionary activity in Palestine and Transjordan was the Church Missionary Society. The first achievement of this society, as far as the Arab world was concerned, was the establishment of a printing press in Malta in 1815, to print Bibles and religious tracts in Arabic. The Church Missionary Society next began its activity in Egypt in 1820; and when its work there was interrupted for a period of some years for political reasons, starting in 1840, the society moved to Palestine, founding an Anglican bishopric in Jerusalem in 1841. This made Jerusalem the centre of Anglican missionary activity in the area: an activity which attracted Christian Arabs from both sides of the Jordan – mainly Greek Orthodox or Greek Catholic – to join the Anglican communion in due course. The first bishop of the Arab Anglican communion (subsequently called the Arab Episcopal Church) was Najib Qub'ayn, who was consecrated in 1956. And the communion continues to flourish in Jordan and Palestine/Israel to this day.

While the missionary activity of the Anglicans in Palestine and Transjordan was the work of the Church Missionary Society, that of the Presbyterian and Congregational churches in Syria, Mount Lebanon, Iraq, Egypt and elsewhere was organized and coordinated by the American Board of Commissioners for Foreign Missions. It was through the agency of this board that a Presbyterian 'native church' of Congregational character – what came to be called the National Evangelical Church – was founded in Beirut in 1947, as a self-governing body; and that Presbyterian churches were founded in different Lebanese and Syrian towns and villages, some by American missionaries acting in co-ordination with the Board, others by the initiative of local converts. Initially, the churches founded by the missionaries were kept under the Board's direct supervision. In 1920, however, as the Board began to reduce its missionary operations, a synod of three presbyteries was established for these churches; and in 1958, when the operations of the Board were finally liquidated, all its institutions and properties devolved to the National Evangelical Synod of Syria and Lebanon. The National Evangelical Church of Beirut, however, remains the larger and more important body, its sister church in Syria being the National Evangelical Church of Damascus.

The Protestant churches of Lebanon, Syria, Palestine and Jordan apart, others deserve to be mentioned: among them the largest, which is the Coptic Evangelical Church. Founded by United Presbyterian missionaries from the United States in 1853, and remaining attached to that American church for nearly a century, the Coptic Evangelical Church, organized as the Synod of the Nile, became fully self-governing in 1958, at the same time as the National Evangelical Synod of Syria and Lebanon. Also deserving of mention, despite their small size, are the Arab Evangelical congregations and Assyrian Evangelical congregations of Iraq, both of which are also Presbyterian communions.

In Lebanon and Syria, as in Jordan and Palestine, and also in Iraq, the local Protestant ranks were swelled in time by Armenian Protestants who began to arrive in the Arab lands as refugees, in the wake of the successive massacres suffered by the Armenians in the Turkish provinces of the Ottoman empire, starting in 1894, and more so after 1915. The Armenian Evangelical congregation (today, the Union of Armenian Evangelical Churches in the Near East), again a Presbyterian communion, was originally founded by the American Board of Foreign Missions in Istanbul in 1846.

Apart from the Presbyterians, Anglicans and Lutherans, the Protestants of the Arab world today count small pockets of Quakers, Baptists, Seventh Day Adventists, Church of God followers, and others. Among those, the Quakers, or Friends, are the oldest. The Society of Friends began its missionary activity in Mount Lebanon in the 1870s, then extended its work to Palestine, winning few Arab converts, but making its mark nevertheless by outstanding contributions to education and social work.

11

The Arab Uniates and Protestants
in Retrospect

Viewed in historical perspective, the Roman Catholic and Protestant missionary activity that brought about the establishment of the Uniate and Protestant communions in the Arab world had two effects, the first negative, the second distinctly positive. On the negative side, this missionary activity destroyed the original unity of historical Eastern Christian communions by creating Uniate churches out of each, or by attracting converts to Protestantism from each historical communion. What was left behind, as a result, was a legacy of distrust and quarrels between daughter and mother communities, the former considering the latter to be fossilized and obsolescent; the latter accusing the former of slavish Westernization and treason to the Eastern Chnstian heritage. On the positive side, however, one must bear in mind that the Uniates in each of the traditional Eastern churches separated from the mother church to emerge as new communions with an enhanced rather than weakened sense of ethnic identity. And in the special case of the Melchite church, long dominated on its Arab home grounds by a Greek higher clergy, the Uniate Greek

Catholic church broke away from it, at least partly, in protest against the unjustified Greek domination. From the moment of its establishment as a separate communion, the Greek Catholic church has been run entirely by an Arab clergy, headed by an Arab patriarch. Its emergence, moreover, brought with it the introduction of the first Arabic press to the Arab lands; also, the small beginnings of what was to become the great Arabic literary revival of the nineteenth century. By contrast, the Greek Orthodox, non-Uniate Melchites of the see of Alexandria did not elect a native Egyptian patriarch for themselves until 1846; those of the see of Antioch only managed to elect their first Arab patriarch in 1899; and a Greek patriarch, with a solidly Greek higher clergy, continues to dominate the Greek Orthodox, non-Uniate see of Jerusalem to this day.

In each of the Uniate communions, strong emphasis was consistently laid on the preservation of the rite of the mother church, rather than the adoption of the Latin rite in its place; and minor modifications of rite were only made where the original rite touched upon disputed points of doctrine.

In their work among the various Eastern churches, the Roman Catholic missionaries encouraged them to take pride in their ethnic identity and historical heritage. And the same was done by the Protestant missionaries. In the churches they founded in the Arab lands, the latter missionaries, and particularly the Americans among them, exerted every effort to make Arabic the exclusive language of religious services; and among the most notable achievements of the American Presbyterian mission in Beirut was the translation of the Bible into modern Arabic, and the production of an Arabic hymnal. The Anglican missionaries, for their part, made a point of having an Arabic version made of their Book of Common Prayer. Meanwhile, in the Protestant as in the Uniate schools and colleges, prime stress was laid on the teaching of the Arabic language, and on the production of textbooks on all subjects in Arabic. Small wonder that the idea of Arab nationalism was given its first formulation and articulation by Christian Arabs who were mostly Uniates or Protestants, or ones who had been educated in Uniate or Protestant schools.

12

The Christians in the Modern Arab World

In the Arab world today, Christian communities continue to flourish in Egypt, Iraq, Jordan, Lebanon and Syria, as well as among the Arabs of Palestine/Israel. (In the Arabian peninsula and the countries of North Africa, the resident Christians are mainly Arab or European expatriates; the Sudanese Christians, limited mostly to the southern parts of Sudan, are not of Arab stock.)

Estimates of the total Christian population in the contemporary Arab world vary, some estimates being exaggerated, others tending to be conservative, or even alarmist. A reasonable guess would place the number at approximately ten million, distributed between the different countries more or less as follows (with the approximate percentage of the respective national population indicated in parentheses): in Egypt, about six million (12.5 per cent); in Lebanon, nearly two million (an accepted estimate of 40 per cent); in Syria, nearly one million (perhaps 6 per cent); in Jordan and among the Arabs of Palestine/Israel, half a million (more or less divided between Jordanians and Palestinians, amounting to roughly 6 per cent in each case); in Iraq, half a million (about 3 per cent).

The statistical breakdown of the Christian Arabs by

denomination is also a matter of rough estimate, deriving from church registers which are normally incomplete, and so inaccurate. The largest of the denominations, counting only the members resident in the Arab world, is certainly that of the Copts in Egypt. They are believed to number over five million. The Greek Orthodox, counting a total of approximately one million, and divided between Syria and Lebanon, Jordan and Palestine, follow numerically as a poor second, the largest national group among them being the Syrian. Next come the Maronites, numbering nearly one million and concentrated mainly in Lebanon. The Armenians of the Arab world (Gregorians by the vast majority, but also counting Catholics and Protestants) number a total of approximately 400,000, more than half of them in Lebanon. So do the Greek Catholics, more than half of whom, like the Armenians, are in Lebanon. Other than the Greek Catholics, the one Uniate community of notable size in the Arab world is that of the Chaldeans, numbering about 250,000, the overwhelming majority of them in Iraq. By contrast, the Assyrian Orthodox (or Nestorian) church of Iraq, from which the Chaldean church originally split, has barely 50,000 followers. Other Christian communions of the modern Arab world count no more than a few tens of thousands each, or perhaps 100,000 or 120,000 at the most (as in the case of the Syrian Orthodox church). The Arab Roman Catholics or 'Latins' belong in this category. The Arab Protestants, on the other hand, number at least 180,000, and perhaps as many as 200,000, all denominations included, of whom more that 130,000 are Egyptian, and perhaps as many as 25,000 Lebanese (in the latter case, counting the Armenian Protestants).

Far more important that the numbers of the Christians in the modern Arab world is their social, economic and cultural visibility, and in some cases, also their political visibility. In the course of the nineteenth century, the Christians of Ottoman Syria (comprising what are today Lebanon, Syria, Palestine, Israel and Jordan) – and, more particularly, the Protestants and Uniate Catholics among them – played the leading role in the Arab renaissance of that period. A galaxy of eminent scholars emerged from their ranks at the time, effecting a remarkable revival of Arabic humanism, and laying the intellectual foundations for the idea of Arab nationalism, as already observed. Meanwhile, Syrian Christian expatriates in Egypt, coming from Mount Lebanon as from other parts, pioneered in modern Arab journalism, founding newspapers and scientific and literary periodicals, and virtually creating the modern Arab press. Also, throughout the Arab world, Christian Arabs pioneered during that period in the learned professions, and also in education. In all their achievements, they set examples for others to follow. But what set the pioneering Christians of those times socially and intellectually ahead of their Muslim compatriots was the fact that, unlike their Muslim contemporaries, they had no inhibitions about accepting new ideas and social models coming from the Western world – a world with which they symbolically shared their Christianity.

With the emergence of the contemporary Arab world in the wake of the First World War, one Christian Arab community – the Maronites – played the leading role in the creation and political maintenance of the Lebanese Republic. Christians of different denominations also played prominent roles in the politics of other emerging

Arab countries where they happened to be found: Egypt, Syria, Iraq, Jordan and now Palestine. Being naturally attuned to the ethos of the West, Christian Arabs who happened to be articulate were ideally suited to present the positions of their respective countries – also, the Arab national position in general, on whatever issue – on international platforms. And this they have normally been entrusted to do by unanimous Arab consent. Until the present day, Christians remain leading spokesmen for Arab national causes – most notably, the Palestinian Arab cause.

Much concern about the future of the Christian Arabs is currently being expressed in international circles and the international media. Also, much fear of the future is being voiced among Christians inside the Arab world, particularly in connection with the waves of Islamic fundamentalism which have been sweeping a number of Arab countries during the last decade. People who entertain such concern or fear rarely take into account that it is in the nature of waves, no matter their apparent enormity, to subside once they have consumed their initial driving force, especially in the case of waves of social behaviour driven by ephemeral emotion rather than by solid reason. The fact remains that the Christian Arabs are in no way aliens to Muslim Arab society: a society whose history and culture they have shared for over fourteen centuries to date, without interruption, and to whose material and moral civilization they have continually contributed, and eminently so, on their own initiative or by trustful request.

With such a heritage of trust and good faith in their favour, Christian Arabs need not feel any more apprehensive than other Arabs of things to come. With the patience, resilience and empathy for which they have been historically known, and the imaginative leadership they have rarely lacked, they will surely not be at a loss to find their place in the Arab world of the future, to their own benefit, and to the benefit of all other parties concerned.

PRINCIPAL CHRISTIAN CONFESSIONS AND CHURCHES

Ante-Nicene Christianity

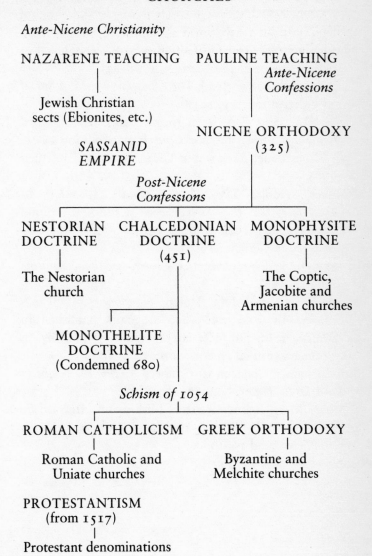

NAZARENE TEACHING

Jewish Christian
sects (Ebionites, etc.)

PAULINE TEACHING

*Ante-Nicene
Confessions*

NICENE ORTHODOXY
(325)

*SASSANID
EMPIRE*

*Post-Nicene
Confessions*

NESTORIAN
DOCTRINE

The Nestorian
church

CHALCEDONIAN
DOCTRINE
(451)

MONOPHYSITE
DOCTRINE

The Coptic,
Jacobite and
Armenian churches

MONOTHELITE
DOCTRINE
(Condemned 680)

Schism of 1054

ROMAN CATHOLICISM

Roman Catholic and
Uniate churches

GREEK ORTHODOXY

Byzantine and
Melchite churches

PROTESTANTISM
(from 1517)

Protestant denominations

Bibliography

Aland, Kurt, *A History of Christianity*, 2 vols (1985–86; originally published in German, 1980–82).

Barraclough, Geoffrey (ed.), *The Christian World: A Social and Cultural History* (1918).

Cross, F.L. and E.A. Livingstone (eds.), *The Oxford Dictionary of the Christian Church*, third edition 1997.

Fox, Robin Lane, *Pagans and Christians* (1986, reissued 1988).

Harnack, Adolf, *The Mission and Expansion of Christianity in the First Three Centuries*, second enlarged and revised edition, 2 vols (1908; originally published in German, 1902).

Hussey, J.M., *The Orthodox Church in the Byzantine Empire* (1986).

Jedin, Hubert and John Dolan, *Handbook of Church History*, 10 vols (1965–81; originally published in German, 1962–79). The later volumes of the English edition are entitled *History of the Church*.

Trimingham, J. Spencer, *Christianity Among the Arabs in Pre-Islamic Times*, London, 1979.

Van Der Meer, F. and Christian Mohrmann, *Atlas of the Early Christian World*, translated from the Dutch (1958, reprinted 1966).

Indexes

A. General Index

B. Foreign terms

C. Biblical citations and references

Genesis		24.36–49	25	Galatians	
2.24	28			1.12	6
17.9–14	5	John		1.13	4
		1.1–18	3	1.13–14	6
Exodus		20.21–22	25	2.6–10	11
5.1–22	5			3.23–25	6
20.4–5	43	Acts			
		8.17	25	Ephesians	
Isaiah		11.26	32	2.8–9	78
60.3	3, 8	11.30	26	5.31–33	28
		14.23	26		
Matthew		22.25–29	11	Philippians	
1.1–16	8	23.27	11	1.1	26
1.18–2	8				
16.18–19	18, 32	Romans		I Timothy	
26.26–29	13	1.17	78	1.5	26
26.28	4	2.28–29	6	3.1	26
28.16–20	25	10.9	19	3.16	18
28.19	3, 18	10.10	7	3.8–13	26
28.20	1	13.1–6	12	4.14	26
				5.17	26
Mark		I Corinthians			
14.22–25	13	11.23–26	13	II Timothy	
14.24	4	11.25	4	1.7	26
16.14–18	25			2.11–13	26
		II Corinthians			
Luke		3.6	4	I John	
2.1–7	8	3.14	4	1.8–9	29
3.23–31	8	12.1 b–4	6		
22.14–20	13	13.13	3, 18	II Peter	
22.20	4			3.15–16	13